THE
EVERYTHING®
ESSENTIAL GERMAN
BOOK

Dear Reader,

Learning a foreign language can be a rewarding endeavor, especially when you truly want to know the language and make the choice in order to achieve some personal goal. And I'm glad your choice is German. It's an important world language that is rich in history and culture.

Whether you want to be a German translator or just an informed tourist cruising down the Rhine or strolling along Kurfürstendamm in Berlin, you'll find *The Everything® Essential German Book* the perfect vehicle for getting started on your linguistic journey. A language is much more than grammar rules and vocabulary lists. It's also the means for transmitting traditions and maintaining a culture's sensibilities. This book provides the "essentials" of all these elements and is a handy resource for reviewing them quickly. When practicing new phrases, be sure to say them out loud, even when you write them. Remember, you don't just "think" a language; it's first and foremost a spoken entity.

I think you'll find that learning German can be fun and exciting. After you've developed your skills, your new language will be a helpful tool in discovering the world beyond our country's borders. Have fun. *Viel Spaß!*

Sincerely,

Edward Swick

D0112325

Welcome to the EVERYTHING Series!

These handy, accessible books give you all you need to tackle a difficult project, gain a new hobby, or even brush up on something you learned back in school but have since forgotten. You can choose to read from cover to cover or just pick out information from our four useful boxes.

 Alerts

Urgent warnings

 Facts

Important snippets of information

 **Essentials**

Quick handy tips

 **Questions**

Answers to common questions

When you're done reading, you can finally say you know **EVERYTHING®**!

PUBLISHER Karen Cooper

MANAGING EDITOR, EVERYTHING® SERIES Lisa Laing

COPY CHIEF Casey Ebert

ASSOCIATE PRODUCTION EDITOR Mary Beth Dolan

ACQUISITIONS EDITOR Lisa Laing

DEVELOPMENT EDITOR Eileen Mullan

EVERYTHING® SERIES COVER DESIGNER Erin Alexander

Visit the entire Everything® series at *www.everything.com*

THE
EVERYTHING®
ESSENTIAL GERMAN BOOK

All you need to learn German in no time

Edward Swick, MA

Avon, Massachusetts

Copyright © 2013 by F+W Media, Inc.
All rights reserved.
This book, or parts thereof, may not be reproduced in any form without
permission from the publisher; exceptions are made for brief excerpts used in
published reviews.

An Everything® Series Book.
Everything® and everything.com® are registered trademarks of F+W Media, Inc.

Published by Adams Media, a division of F+W Media, Inc.
57 Littlefield Street, Avon, MA 02322. U.S.A.
www.adamsmedia.com

Contains material adapted and abridged from *The Everything® Learning German
Book* by Edward Swick, copyright © 2009 by F+W Media, Inc., ISBN 10: 1-59869-
989-X, ISBN 13: 978-1-59869-989-0.

ISBN 10: 1-4405-6757-3
ISBN 13: 978-1-4405-6757-5
eISBN 10: 1-4405-6758-1
eISBN 13: 978-1-4405-6758-2

Printed in the United States of America.

10   9   8   7   6   5   4   3   2   1

Many of the designations used by manufacturers and sellers to distinguish their
products are claimed as trademarks. Where those designations appear in this
book and F+W Media was aware of a trademark claim, the designations have
been printed with initial capital letters.

*This book is available at quantity discounts for bulk purchases.
For information, please call 1-800-289-0963.*

Contents

Introduction

It's always a good time to learn a new language! Perhaps you want to know German for business purposes, or you want to travel in the German-speaking countries. Maybe you have a keen interest in German literature and no longer want to read translations. Or maybe you're interested in Germany itself because Grandpa Schmidt came from Bavaria eighty years ago and you just have to know more about his hometown and your family history.

No matter what your goal is in learning German, right now is the perfect time to start, and *The Everything® Essential German Book* gives you all the basics you need to know. With a lot of enthusiasm and a little self-discipline, you can soon be on your way to acquiring the skills you need to speak and understand German.

German and English are brother and sister languages. At an early age they became separated and were brought up in different locations: the brother on the continent, the sister in England. This relationship makes learning German a relatively comfortable experience for English speakers, because there are many words and elements in both languages that are still quite similar.

The word *language* comes from the Latin *lingua*, which means "tongue." That's an important fact. Articulating utterances by moving the tongue inside the mouth creates the sounds that we call language. Language is, therefore, fundamentally a spoken form. And when you use this book, you should discipline yourself to practice everything you learn out loud. Just "thinking" a new phrase or writing it down isn't enough. You have to practice speaking German to learn German well.

The contents of each chapter will guide you smoothly to understanding new structures and words. They are designed like building blocks. Understanding Concept A will help you learn Concept B. Understanding Concept B will help you learn Concept C, and so on. And you can move from idea to idea as slowly or as rapidly as is comfortable for you. The choice of a timetable for acquiring your German skills is yours.

If this is your first attempt at learning a foreign language, you will probably be surprised at just how simple the process is. If you know other foreign languages, you will discover that *The Everything® Essential German Book* is an efficient vehicle for developing your next language—German.

With new language skills, you open up many new avenues for yourself. The number of books available to you will be vastly increased. You'll have access to a wider range of magazines and newspapers and, thereby, to new points of view. There will be more movies and theater productions to enjoy. And you will no longer be limited to meeting and getting to know only people who speak English. It will truly help to make you what the Germans call *ein Weltbürger*—a citizen of the world.

However you approach this learning experience, enjoy yourself. Experiment with words. Be creative with what you know. As long as you are consistent and enthusiastic, you will succeed. Have fun! *Viel Spaß!*

CHAPTER 1

German Pronunciation

Pronouncing German words is fairly straightforward, and most English speakers find that they have little difficulty learning German pronunciation. The following sections will guide you through what you need to know to start pronouncing German like a native.

Cognates in Context

There are so many shortcuts to learning new German words. The following few sentences use some words that will probably look familiar to you. Don't worry about understanding the sentence structure yet. Just use these sentences to get used to looking at written German. Can you pick out the meanings of any of the words?

Andreas gewinnt einen Preis.	Andreas wins a prize.
Meine Familie ist sehr klein.	My family is very small.
Wir lieben die Natur.	We love nature.
Das ist perfekt!	That's perfect!
Er braucht Salz und Pfeffer.	He needs salt and pepper.
Deine Schwester ist sehr attraktiv.	Your sister is very attractive.
Warum bist du so nervös?	Why are you so nervous?
Ich trinke keinen Kaffee.	I don't drink coffee.
Jazz ist sehr populär.	Jazz is very popular.

 **Essential**

If you treat every German word you find here as a spoken form, you will learn how to read and speak the language more easily. Say every word and every phrase you encounter out loud. If you're not saying them accurately or smoothly, practice them out loud until you can.

The Alphabet

The German alphabet (*das Alphabet*) consists of the same letters that make up our English alphabet, with one exception. German has one letter that we do not have in English. It is called an "ess-tset" and is often mistaken for a capital *B*. It looks like this (*ß*) and is pronounced like a double *s* (ESS). It takes the place of *ss* after long vowels and diphthongs. Note these examples: *heißen, süß, weiß.*

▼ **DAS ALPHABET**

Letter	Pronunciation	Letter	Pronunciation
A a	*ah*	O o	*oh*
Ä ä	*ah umlaut*	Ö ö	*oh umlaut*
B b	*bay*	P p	*pay*
C c	*tsay*	Q q	*koo*
D d	*day*	R r	*air*
E e	*ay*	S s	*ess*
F f	*eff*	T t	*tay*
G g	*gay*	U u	*oo*
H h	*ha*	Ü ü	*oo umlaut*
I i	*ee*	V v	*fow*
J j	*yawt*	W w	*vay*
K k	*kah*	X x	*ix*
L l	*ell*	Y y	*uepsilon*
M m	*em*	Z z	*tset*
N n	*en*		

Pronouncing the Vowels

The following descriptions can serve as your guide as you practice forming German sounds. The English phonetics are enclosed in parentheses with the stressed syllable in capital letters—for example, *Vater* (FAH-tuh).

 Alert

Be aware that the English pronunciation is an approximation of the German sound and not always a perfect replica of it. Listening to German radio, television, and films will give you a better sense of the sounds as pronounced by native Germans.

When English phonetics are provided, there is no precise way to indicate the pronunciation of *Ö ö* and *Ü ü*. The phonetics will show their sounds as *er* (in bold letters) and *ue* (in bold letters) respectively.

An umlaut is the two dots that sometimes appear over the letters *a*, *o*, and *u*. They occur with no other letters. As you'll see in the following table, the umlaut changes the pronunciation of the vowel sound slightly.

▼ PRONOUNCING THE VOWEL SOUNDS

Letter	Sound	Example	Pronunciation	Translation
A a	*ah* as in "father"	*Vater*	(FAH tuh)	father
Ä ä	*ay* as in "say"	*spät*	(SHPATE)	late
E e	*ay* as in "say"	*Weg*	(VAYK)	path
I i	*ee* as in "tree"	*ich*	(EE**CH**)	I
O o	*o* as in "go"	*Foto*	(FOE-toe)	photo
Ö ö	*e* as in "her"	*schön*	(SHERN)	beautiful
U u	*oo* as in "moon"	*tut*	(TOOT)	does
Ü ü	pucker lips to say *oo* but say *ee*	*Tür*	(T**U**R)	door
Y y	pucker lips to say *oo* but say *ee*	*Gymnasium*	(G**U**EM-nah-zee-oom)	high school

Long and Short Vowels

Just as in English, there is a slight difference between long and short vowels in German. The words "long" and "short" are an accurate description of the difference between the sounds in German. Long vowels are drawn out more when pronounced. They tend to precede a single consonant. Short vowels usually precede a double consonant and are pronounced more quickly. For example, the long German *a* is pronounced *ah*; the short German *a* is pronounced *uh*. A rare exception to this rule is the article *das* (DUSS).

▼ **LONG VOWEL SOUNDS BEFORE A SINGLE CONSONANT**

German Word	Pronunciation of Vowel	Pronunciation of Word	Translation
Vater	long *ah*	(FAH-tuh)	father
Käse	long *ay*	(KAY-zeh)	cheese
Keks	long *ay*	(KAYKS)	cookie
grob	long *oh*	(GROP)	rude, rough
schön	long *er*	(SH**ER**N)	beautiful
gut	long *oo*	(GOOT)	good
spülen	long *oo* umlaut	(SHP**UE**-len)	to flush

▼ **SHORT VOWEL SOUNDS BEFORE A DOUBLE CONSONANT**

German Word	Pronunciation of Vowel	Pronunciation of Word	Translation
Halle	short *uh*	(HUH-leh)	hall
fällen	short *eh*	(FELL-en)	to chop down
Keller	short *eh*	(KELL-uh)	basement
Zoll	short *aw*	(TSAWL)	customs
können	short *er*	(K**ER**-nen)	to be able to
Mummel	short *oo*	(MOOM-ell)	water lily
müssen	short *oo* umlaut	(M**UE**SS-en)	to have to

Look at the form of a word to determine whether the phonetic spelling *oo* is long or short: *Mutter* (MOO-tuh) (short *oo* because it precedes a double consonant) or *tun* (TOON) (long *oo* because it precedes a single consonant).

Pronouncing the Consonants

German consonants are pronounced fairly close to how they are pronounced in English. The following table shows you how to pronounce the consonants in German words.

▼ PRONOUNCING THE CONSONANTS

Letter	Pronunciation	Example	Pronunciation	Translation
B b	*b* as in "baby"	*Buch*	(BOO**CH**)	book
C c	*ts* as in "bits"	*CD*	(tsay DAY)	CD (occurs primarily in foreign words)
D d	*d* as in "did"	*Doktor*	(DAWK-tuh)	doctor
F f	*f* as in "fit"	*fein*	(FINE)	fine
G g	*g* as in "goggles"	*gut*	(GOOT)	good
H h	*h* as in "hat"	*Haus*	(HOUSE)	house
J j	*y* as in "yard"	*ja*	(YAH)	yes
K k	*k* as in "kick"	*Kind*	(KINT)	child
L l	*l* as in "little"	*bellen*	(BELL-en)	to bark
M m	*m* as in "mama"	*Mutter*	(MOO-tuh)	mother
N n	*n* as in "noon"	*nicht*	(NIH**CH**T)	not
P p	*p* as in "papa"	*Preis*	(PRICE)	prize
Q q	*kv* as in "bac**k v**ent"	*Quelle*	(KVELL-eh)	source
R r	guttural similar to French *r* or rolled similar to Italian *r*	*rot*	(ROT)	red
S s	*s* as in "sis" (middle of a word)	*Meister*	(MYE-stuh)	master
S s	*z* as in "zap" (start of a word)	*soll*	(ZAWL)	ought to
T t	*t* as in "toot"	*tun*	(TOON)	to do
V v	*eff* as in "fit"	*vier*	(FEER)	four

Letter	Pronunciation	Example	Pronunciation	Translation
V v	*v* as in "very" (usually foreign words)	*Vase*	(VAH-zeh)	vase
W w	*v* as in "Vivian"	*Walter*	(VAHL-tuh)	the name Walter
X x	*x* as in "wax"	*verflixt*	(fare-FLIKST)	tricky
Z z	*ts* as in "bits"	*Zoll*	(TSAWL)	customs

There are a few things you have to look out for with certain conso-nants, besides what's given in the previous table. Sometimes the con-sonants change sound depending on their placement in a word, as you can already see from the pronunciation for the letter *s*. When the letter *b* appears at the end of a word or prefix, it is pronounced like a *p*. When the letter *d* appears at the end of a word or prefix, it is pronounced like a *t*.

▼ SOUNDING THE LETTER *B* AT THE END OF A WORD OR PREFIX

German	Pronunciation	English
grob	(GROP)	rude, rough
starb	(SHTAHRP)	died
ablehnen	(AHP-lay-nen)	to reject
absagen	(AHP-zah-gen)	to cancel

▼ SOUNDING THE LETTER *D* AT THE END OF A WORD OR PREFIX

German	Pronunciation	English
Deutschland	(DOITCH-lunt)	Germany
Freund	(FROINT)	friend
Kind	(KINT)	child
Gold	(GAWLT)	gold
Geld	(GELT)	money
Bild	(BILLT)	picture

When the letter *g* appears at the end of a word or prefix, it is pro-nounced like a *k*. However, when it follows the letter *n* it is pronounced like the English *ng*: *jung* (YOONG) young.

▼ **SOUNDING THE LETTER G AT THE END OF A WORD OR PREFIX**

German	Pronunciation	English
Weg	(VAYK)	path
lag	(LAHK)	lay
trug	(TROOK)	wore
weglaufen	(VEHK-low-fen)	to run away

In 1998, Germany adopted new spelling rules to try to simplify the language as it is taught in schools. The most obvious change involves the use of the ß in words—ß is to be used only after long vowels and diphthongs, and ss is to be used following short vowel sounds. So daß becomes dass under the new rules. Until 2005 both spellings were accepted, but now the new spellings are the only officially acceptable ones.

Letter Combinations

German pronunciation is also affected by groups of letters. Certain combinations of letters have their own sounds that you must be aware of. When two vowels in the same syllable form one speech sound, it is called a diphthong.

▼ **PRONOUNCING COMBINED LETTERS AND DIPHTHONGS**

Letter Combination	Sound	Example	Pronunciation	English
AA	ah as in "father"	Saal	(ZAHL)	hall, saloon
AU	ow as in "cow"	Frau	(FROW)	woman
EU	oi as in "toil"	Heu	(HOI)	hay
ÄU	oi as in "toil"	Fräulein	(FROI-line)	young woman
EI	i as in "high"	klein	(KLINE)	small
IE	ee as in "feet"	tief	(TEEF)	deep
EE	ay as in "say"	Tee	(TAY)	tea
ER	air as in "stair"	merken	(MAIR-ken)	to notice

Letter Combination	Sound	Example	Pronunciation	English
ER	*uh* as in British "fath**er**" (end of word only)	*Messer*	(MESS-uh)	knife
OO	*o* as in "home"	*Boot*	(BOTE)	boat
CH	soft *ch* similar to *h* in "human"	*ich*	(EE**CH**)	I
CH	guttural *ch* as in Scottish "loch"	*Koch*	(KO**CH**)	cook
CHS	*x* as in "wax"	*sechs*	(ZEHKS)	six
SCH	*sh* as in "shush"	*Schuh*	(SHOO)	shoe
TSCH	*ch* as in "church"	*Deutschland*	(DOITCH-lunt)	Germany
SP	*shp* as in "ca**sh p**ayment"	*Sport*	(SHPORT)	sport
ST	*sht* as in "wa**sh t**ub"	*stark*	(SHTAHRK)	strong
TH	*t* as in "Tom"	*Bibliothek*	(beeb-lee-oh-TAKE)	library
PF	*pf* as in "to**p f**in"	*Pfennig*	(PFENN-ik)	penny
TZ	*ts* as in "its"	*Hitze*	(HITS-eh)	heat

Many words in German have an *h* directly following a vowel. That *h* is most often silent. For example, *gehen* (to go) is not (GAY-hen). It is pronounced (GAY-en).

Note also that the German soft *ch* is used commonly after the vowels *e, i, ei, ie, eu, äu,* and *ö*. The guttural *ch* is used generally after the vowels *a, ä, o, u, ü,* and *au*.

▼ **PRONOUNCING WORDS WITH AN *H* FOLLOWING A VOWEL**

German	Pronunciation	English
fliehen	(FLEE-en)	to flee
glühen	(GL**UE**-en)	to make red hot
sehen	(ZAY-en)	to see
stehen	(SHTAY-en)	to stand

There is no English equivalent for German *ch* (guttural like Scottish *ch* in "loch"). Both the soft and guttural *ch* will be shown phonetically as **ch** (in bold letters) and should not be confused with the English version of that letter combination. An umlaut is the two dots placed over the letters *a, o,* and *u. Ä ä* is pronounced much like *ay.* But *Ö ö* and *Ü ü* have pronunciations that do not occur in English. *Ö ö* sounds much like *er* and *Ü ü* sounds like *ue* said with pursed lips. Both will appear in the phonetics in bold as **er** and **ue** respectively.

Practicing Your Pronunciation

Use the following list of words to practice your German pronunciation. Try to sound out the words without looking at the phonetic spelling at first, then check to see if you are right.

▼ **VOCABULARY WORDS TO HELP YOU PRACTICE PRONOUNCING GERMAN**

German	Pronunciation	English
absagen	(AHP-zah-gen)	to cancel
Alpen	(ULL-pen)	Alps
alt	(ULT)	old
Amerika	(uh-MAY-ree-kuh)	America
bekam	(bay-KAHM)	received
Berlin	(bare-LEEN)	Berlin
Bild	(BILLT)	picture
Bilder	(BILL-duh)	pictures
brechen	(BRE**CH**-en)	to break
Brüder	(BR**UE**-duh)	brothers

German	Pronunciation	English
Buch	(BOO**CH**)	book
Bücher	(B**UECH**-uh)	books
Deutschland	(DOITCH-lunt)	Germany
Erhardt	(AIR-hart)	the name Erhardt
essen	(ESS-en)	to eat
Frankreich	(FRAHNK-rye**ch**)	France
Fräulein	(FROI-line)	young woman
führen	(F**UE**-ren)	to lead
geht	(GATE)	goes
halten	(HULL-ten)	to hold
Hamburg	(HAHM-boork)	Hamburg
Händel	(HENN-del)	Händel
Insel	(IN-zel)	island
jung	(YOONG)	young
Junker	(YOONK-uh)	titled landowner
Kanada	(KAHN-nah-dah)	Canada
kaufen	(KOW-fen)	to buy
König	(K**ER**-nik)	king
konnte	(KAWN-teh)	could
kurz	(KOORTZ)	short
lachen	(LUH-**ch**en)	to laugh
lang	(LUNG)	long
langsam	(LUNG-zum)	slow
Leiter	(LYE-tuh)	leader
Löffel	(L**ER**-fel)	spoon
Mann	(MUNN)	man
München	(M**UE**N-**ch**en)	Munich
Mutter	(MOO-tuh)	mother
Nacht	(NAH**CHT**)	night
nicht	(NIH**CHT**)	not
Niedersachsen	(NEE-duh-sux-en)	Lower Saxony
oder	(OH-duh)	or
Panzer	(PUNTS-uh)	tank
Pfeffer	(PFEFF-uh)	pepper
Präsident	(pray-zee-DENT)	president

German	Pronunciation	English
Pulver	(POOL-fuh)	powder
quälen	(KVAY-len)	to torment
Qualität	(kvah-lee-TATE)	quality
reich	(RYE**CH**)	rich
Russland	(ROOS-lunt)	Russia
scheu	(SHOY)	shy
Schnee	(SHNAY)	snow
schnell	(SHNELL)	fast
schön	(SH**ER**N)	beautiful
schwarz	(SHVARTZ)	black
Schwester	(SHVESS-tuh)	sister
Spitze	(SHPITZ-eh)	point
sterben	(SHTAIR-ben)	to die
süß	(**ZU**ESS)	sweet
Türen	(**TUE**-ren)	doors
typisch	(**TUE**P-ish)	typical
über	(**UE**-buh)	over
unter	(OON-tuh)	under
vierzehn	(FEAR-tsayn)	fourteen
voll	(FAWL)	full
weiß	(VICE)	white
Welt	(VELT)	world
Wetter	(VEH-tuh)	weather
wichtig	(VI**CH**-tik)	important
wissen	(VISS-en)	to know
wunderbar	(VOON-duh-bah)	wonderful
zu	(TSOO)	to, too
Zucker	(TSOO-kuh)	sugar

CHAPTER 2

Getting Started with the Basics

What do you need to know to start a conversation? This chapter covers the basics of how to greet someone, introduce yourself, ask someone's name, and ask how he or she is doing. You're on your way to having your first conversation in German!

Names and Titles

Just like English speakers, Germans address one another with first names on an informal basis and with a title and last name on a formal basis. German has shortened first names or nicknames just as English does. *Johann* is known to his friends as *Hans. Margarethe* is *Gretchen* or *Gretel. Eduard* becomes *Edu. Geli* comes from *Angelika.* And sometimes a double first name borrows a syllable from each name to form a nickname: *Lieselotte* becomes *Lilo.*

Essential

German first names—just like English first names—come into fashion and in time fall out of fashion. A popular name with one generation is considered old-fashioned in another. The names you'll encounter in this book will run the gamut: Some will be contemporary and others will be traditional.

You should be aware of such shortened names or nicknames, but don't try using them until you have more experience with the language. Although the English name Richard is also the German name *Richard*, you cannot refer to *Richard* as *Dick*. The German word *dick* means "fat"!

When addressing someone by their last name, you should use the appropriate title of the person to whom you are speaking.

▼ **TITLES IN GERMAN NAMES**

German	Pronunciation	English Equivalent
Herr	(HAIR)	Mr.
Frau	(FROW)	Ms.
Doktor	(DAWK-tuh)	Doctor (academic)
Professor	(proh-FESS-uh)	Professor

Nowadays, you should address all women as *Frau*—married, single, young, and old. As a foreigner, you'll be forgiven if you forget and say *Fräulein*, but it's only polite to strive to use the correct form.

Hello!

To say "hello" to someone, you use the phrase *Guten Tag* (GOO-ten TAHCK). For example, when saying hello to Andreas, you would say, *Guten Tag, Andreas. Guten Tag* literally means "good day." You have probably heard this common German greeting before. But it's typically used to greet someone only during the afternoon. At other times of the day you have to say something else.

 Fact

Even when encountering a group of people, a German will shake the hand of every person in that group—usually even the children. He or she will say, *Guten Tag, Ilse*, and shake her hand. And so on with *Hans*, *Andreas*, *Maria*, *Professor Klein*, and little *Sabine*.

In the morning you should say *Guten Morgen* (MAWR-gen), which means "good morning." In the afternoon you say *Guten Tag*. In the evening use *Guten Abend* (AH-bent), which means "good evening." And late at night you say *Gute Nacht* (NAH**CH**T), or "good night," which, just as in English, is a way of saying "good-bye" but also means "good night" when you are going to bed.

Good-bye!

Most English speakers already know that Germans say good-bye with the phrase *auf Wiedersehen* (OWF VEE-duh-zane). But it really doesn't mean "good-bye." A closer translation is "till I see you again."

There is another form of good-bye that is very commonly used, although mostly among good friends. It is very casual. It originated a long time ago when it was fashionable to use a French word when bidding farewell to friends: *Adieu*. In the course of time, and with people from all over the German-speaking world pronouncing and mispronouncing the word, it somehow got an *s* attached to it. Then it lost its first syllable. In time it became simply *Tschüs* (CH**UE**SS).

You can't go wrong by saying *auf Wiedersehen*, but it's fun using *Tschüs* when the occasion allows for it: in casual circumstances or when saying good-bye to friends.

When you say that someone is going home, use the following phrase:

Andreas geht jetzt nach Hause.
(ahn-DRAY-us GATE YETZT NAH**CH** HOW-zeh)
(Andreas is going home now.)

When someone is going home, it's an appropriate time to wish him or her *auf Wiedersehen* or *Tschüs*.

If you're speaking on the phone, you don't use *auf Wiedersehen* to say good-bye. That's only for when you see someone face-to-face. When saying good-bye on the phone, use auf *Wiederhören* (OWF VEE-duh-h**er**-ren). It means something like "till I hear your voice again."

How Are You?

When asking how someone is doing, you first have to decide whether you're on a casual or formal basis with the person. Usually, if you're using someone's first name, you have a casual or informal relationship. If you're using a title and last name, you have a formal relationship.

Casual: "How are you?" *"Wie geht's, Andreas?"* (VEE GATES)
Formal: "How are you?" *"Wie geht es Ihnen, Herr Braun?"* (VEE GATE ESS EE-nen)

 Fact

> The word *geht's* is actually a contraction of two words: *geht es*. *Geht es* can be used in place of the contraction. One response to this question is *Es geht mir gut* (ESS GATE MEER GOOT): "It's going well."

Exercise 2-1

Fill in the blank with the appropriate form of asking how someone is in the formal or casual form: *Wie geht es Ihnen?* or *Wie geht's?*

1. _____ , *Professor Braun?*
2. _____ , *Angelika?*
3. _____ , *Hans?*
4. _____ , *Frau Keller?*
5. _____ , *Herr Doktor?*

Some Important New Words

With a few new words, you will be able to form more intricate German sentences. These will help you in basic conversations and simple dialogues. Up until now you have encountered words that are very similar to English words. But as some of the following examples show, the meaning of many German words is not always obvious.

German	Pronunciation	English
wie	(VEE)	how
es	(ESS)	it
wo	(VOH)	where
gut	(GOOT)	good, well
nicht so gut	(NIH**CH**T ZOH GOOT)	not so well
schlecht	(SHLE**CH**T)	bad
hier	(HEAR)	here
da	(DAH)	there
in der Stadt	(IN DAIR SHTUTT)	in the city
nein	(NINE)	no
ja	(YAH)	yes

What Is Your Name?

To ask someone's name, you need to use a special little phrase: *Wie heißen Sie?* (VEE HYE-sen ZEE). Actually, the word "name" isn't even in the phrase. The meaning of the phrase is closer to "What are you called?"

When you meet someone new and wish to learn his or her name, this is the phrase you should use. The response is quite simple: *Ich heiße . . .* (**EECH** HYE-seh), or "My name is . . . " You fill in the blank with the appropriate name. When responding with a last name, it's common to offer the first name, too, just as we often do in English. Look at these examples.

Wie heißen Sie?	*Ich heiße Karl.*
Wie heißen Sie?	*Ich heiße Maria.*
Wie heißen Sie?	*Ich heiße Braun, Herbert Braun.*
Wie heißen Sie?	*Ich heiße Schmidt, Peter Schmidt.*

If you believe you already know someone's name but aren't sure, you can ask about his or her name by placing the verb (*heißen*) in front of the subject (*Sie*): "*Heißen Sie Sabine?*"

The response could be either positive (*ja*) or negative (*nein*). Look at the following possibilities.

Heißen Sie Martin? Ja, ich heiße Martin.
Is your name Martin? Yes, my name is Martin.

Heißen Sie Schröder? Nein, ich heiße Schäfer, Angelika Schäfer.
Is your name Schröder? No, my name is Schäfer, Angelika Schäfer.

Now you are ready to look around and ask the name of someone you see but do not know: "What is the man's name?" "What is the student's name?" In this question the word *heißen* will end in a *t*: *heißt*. "*Wie heißt der Mann?*" "*Wie heißt die Studentin?*"

Exercise 2-2

Ask what someone's name is using the first word in each pair. Respond with the name that is second in the pair. For example, if the first words in the pair are *der Mann*, ask yourself, *Wie heißt der Mann?* (What's the man's name?) Then use the second name in the pair to respond: *Der Mann heißt Andreas.* (The man's name is Andreas.)

1. *die Frau/Maria Schmidt*

_____

2. *der Student* (the male student)/*Karl*

_____

3. *die Studentin* (the female student)/*Anna*

_____

4. *der Ausländer* (foreigner)/*Tom Smith*

_____

CHAPTER 3

First Things First

B y now you may have noticed that nouns often have a *der*, *die*, or *das* before them. What does this mean? In the following sections you'll learn that all nouns have gender, and that all nouns are capitalized. You will also learn about definite and indefinite articles. These are the building blocks for your German vocabulary.

Understanding Gender

In the English language, "gender" refers to the sex of living things: Males are of the masculine gender and females are of the feminine gender. Inanimate objects are called neuter. German is a bit different.

In general, German looks at words that represent males as masculine and words that represent females as feminine. But gender is not entirely based on sex. It is related to custom or how a word is formed, rather than the sexual gender involved.

Der is used frequently with males: *der Vater*, *der Professor*, *der Student*. *Die* is used frequently with females: *die Mutter*, *die Frau*, *die Tante* (aunt). But that's where it ends, because the three genders, denoted by the articles *der*, *die*, and *das*, depend more on word formation than anything else to determine what is masculine, feminine, or neuter.

Masculine nouns, which use *der* as their definite article, do not necessarily refer to males. Likewise, feminine nouns, which use *die* as their definite article, do not always refer to females. And neuter nouns, which use *das* as their definite article, do not refer exclusively to inanimate objects.

The Masculine Nouns

Although there will be exceptions, there are some broad rules for determining the gender of a noun. These rules are helpful guideposts for making intelligent choices when using *der, die,* or *das.*

Here are four basic categories of masculine nouns. (There are more than just four, but these are a good starting point.) Many—but not all!—words that end in *–er, –el,* or *–en* tend to be masculine. In addition, cognates that refer to men also tend to be masculine. Look at the examples in the following table.

▼ **DETERMINING THE GENDER OF COGNATES THAT REFER TO MEN**

Nouns Ending in *–er*	Nouns Ending in *–el*	Nouns Ending in *–en*	Cognates
der Vater (father)	*der Onkel* (uncle)	*der Laden* (store, shop)	*der Professor*
der Lehrer (teacher)	*der Löffel* (spoon)	*der Wagen* (car)	*der Diplomat*
der Keller (cellar)	*der Sattel* (saddle)	*der Magen* (stomach)	*der Tourist*

Notice that half of the words listed above are inanimate objects, but all the words are masculine. Additionally, nouns ending in *–ling, –ig,* and *–ich* are always masculine.

der Frühling (spring)
der Neuling (novice, beginner)
der Sperling (sparrow)
der König (king)
der Teppich (rug, carpet)

Many words of one syllable that end in a consonant are masculine.

der Arzt (doctor)
der Brief (letter)
der Bus (bus)
der Film (film)

der Sohn (son)
der Stuhl (chair)
der Tag (day)
der Tisch (table)

der Freund (male friend)	*der Wein* (wine)
der Markt (market)	*der Zug* (train)
der Park (park)	*der Platz* (market square, place, theater seat)

 Essential

In German, nouns can be made up of multiple words that are combined to form one "compound" noun. The gender of a compound noun is determined by the last part of the word. For instance, you just learned that *der Tag* is masculine because it is a single syllable word that ends in a consonant. This means the days of the week are also masculine: *der Montag* (Monday), *der Dienstag* (Tuesday), and so on.

The Feminine Nouns

Words that refer exclusively to women are usually feminine. Words that refer to women and inanimate objects ending in –*e* tend to be feminine. Words ending in –*in* are feminine. Words that end in –*ung* are feminine. Look at these examples. Notice that many of these words are inanimate objects, yet they are all feminine.

▼ **DETERMINING THE GENDER OF FEMININE NOUNS**

Words Referring to Women	Words Ending in –*e*	Words Ending in –*in*	Words Ending in –*ung*
die Mutter	*die Tante*	*die Studentin*	*die Prüfung* (test)
die Schwester (sister)	*die Tasse* (cup)	*die Lehrerin* (female teacher)	*die Übung* (exercise)
die Frau	*die Schule* ' (school)	*die Freundin* (girlfriend)	*die Achtung* (attention)

Feminine nouns ending in –*in* usually have a masculine counterpart that does not have that ending. The two forms distinguish males and females who have the same role.

▼ **GENDERED ROLES**

The Male Role	The Female Role
der Arzt (physician)	die Ärztin (physician)
der Freund (boyfriend)	die Freundin (girlfriend)
der Künstler (artist)	die Künstlerin (artist)
der Sänger (singer)	die Sängerin (singer)
der Schüler (pupil)	die Schülerin (pupil)

Additionally, nouns ending in –schaft, –ei, and –tät are always feminine.

die Botschaft (message, embassy)   die Metzgerei (butcher's shop)
die Freundschaft (friendship)   die Qualität (quality)
die Landschaft (landscape)   die Universität (university)
die Bäckerei (bakery)   die Wirtschaft (economy)
die Konditorei (confectioner)   die Wissenschaft (science)

Nouns ending in –heit, –keit, and –ie are always feminine.

die Einsamkeit (loneliness)
die Gesundheit (health)
die Poesie (poetry)

Both German and English have a large number of words that end in –tion.

In German they are always feminine, and they usually have the same meaning as their English counterparts. But the German pronunciation and accentuation of this category of nouns is different from English: Position (poh-zee-tsee-OHN), Situation (zit-oo-ah-tsee-OHN). Look at the following words and pronounce them in German.

die Formation   die Reservation
die Information   die Revolution
die Inspektion   die Situation
die Koalition   die Ventilation
die Konstitution   die Vibration
die Position

The Neuter Nouns

Not all inanimate nouns in German are neuter (*das*). There are patterns to watch for when deciding whether a noun is neuter. Diminutives are always neuter. They end either in *–chen* or *–lein*. Words that end in *–um* or *–ium* are always neuter. Words that begin with the prefix *Ge–* tend to be neuter. Look at these examples. Note that some of these neuter words refer to people rather than to inanimate objects.

▼ NEUTER NOUNS

Diminutive with *–chen* or *–lein*	Ending *–um* or *–ium*	Prefix *Ge–*
das Mädchen (girl)	*das Datum* (date)	*das Gemüse* (vegetables)
das Fräulein (young lady)	*das Studium* (study)	*das Getreide* (grain)
das Brötchen (bread roll)	*das Gymnasium* (prep school, high school)	*das Gespenst* (ghost)

Another category of neuter nouns is infinitives that are used as nouns. These are always neuter.

das Einkommen (income) *das Singen* (singing)
das Essen (food) *das Tanzen* (dancing)
das Schreiben (writing)

Certain categories of words tend to be of one gender. Take note of how the following words are related and of their gender.

▼ CATEGORY OF WORDS SHARING THE SAME GENDER—*DAS METALL* (METAL)

English	German	English	German
aluminum	*das Aluminium*	lead	*das Blei*
brass	*das Messing*	silver	*das Silber*
gold	*das Gold*	tin	*das Zinn*
iron	*das Eisen*		

Exceptions to the Gender Patterns

Since there are exceptions in the various patterns, here are a few to consider.

das Bett (bed)	*das Kind* (child)
das Bier (beer)	*das Konzert* (concert)
das Brot (bread)	*der Junge* (boy)
die Fabel (fable)	*die Schwester* (sister)
das Fahrrad (bike)	*die Tochter* (daughter)
das Flugzeug (airplane)	*das Wasser* (water)
der Franzose (Frenchman)	*das Wetter* (weather)
der Geschmack (taste)	*das Wochenende* (weekend)
das Glas (glass)	*die Wurst* (sausage)

You've learned that many words that end in –*e* are feminine: *die Dame* (lady), *die Tasse* (cup), *die Lampe* (lamp), and so on. But there are several masculine words that end in –*e*, too. Memorize these so you can remember that they don't follow the rule.

▼ **MASCULINE NOUNS ENDING IN –*E***

German Noun	English Meaning
der Alte	old man
der Buchstabe	letter (of the alphabet)
der Franzose	Frenchman
der Hase	hare
der Junge	boy
der Knabe	boy, lad
der Löwe	lion
der Matrose	sailor
der Name	name
der Neffe	nephew
der Ochse	ox

Exceptions to the rules, like those words listed above, will always exist. With these words, you must memorize the gender when you learn the noun.

In German, the definite articles (*der, die,* and *das*) that you learned here are in the nominative case. This simply means that these nouns are acting as the subjects of sentences.

Exercise 3-1

After you have studied the previous patterns, practice choosing the correct gender and saying *der, die,* or *das* with each of the words that follows. For example, when presented with the word *Vater,* you would say *der Vater* because *Vater* (father) is masculine. Write the correct article on the line.

1. *Mantel* (coat) _____
2. *Ausstellung* (exhibition) _____
3. *Gelächter* (laughter) _____
4. *Klasse* (class) _____
5. *Brunnen* (well, source of water) _____
6. *Sprache* (language) _____
7. *Männchen* (little man) _____
8. *Prüfung* (exam) _____
9. *Wissenschaft* (science) _____
10. *Essen* (eating) _____

The Indefinite Article

Just like English, German has definite and indefinite articles. Definite articles refer to specific persons or things (the man, the woman, the child), and indefinite articles refer to persons or things in general (a man, a woman, a child). The articles you have learned so far are the definite articles.

▼ **DEFINITE ARTICLES AND GENDER**

Masculine	Feminine	Neuter	English Meaning
der	*die*	*das*	the

You only have to keep your eye on feminine nouns when choosing the indefinite article. Masculine and neuter nouns have the same form: *ein*. The feminine indefinite article is *eine*.

▼ **INDEFINITE ARTICLES AND GENDER**

Masculine	Feminine	Neuter	English Meaning
ein	*eine*	*ein*	a / an

Look at the following examples to see how they relate to the definite articles.

▼ **COMPARING THE DEFINITE AND INDEFINITE ARTICLES**

Masculine Nouns	Feminine Nouns	Neuter Nouns
der Mann / ein Mann	*die Frau / eine Frau*	*das Kind / ein Kind*
der Laden / ein Laden	*die Klasse / eine Klasse*	*das Studium / ein Studium*
der Onkel / ein Onkel	*die Freundin / eine Freundin*	*das Geschenk / ein Geschenk*

Exercise 3-2

Change the definite article of each noun to the indefinite article. For example, when presented with the word *der Vater*, you would say *ein Vater* to change to the indefinite article.

1. *der Lehrer* (teacher) _____
2. *die Schauspielerin* (actress) _____
3. *die Tasse* (cup) _____
4. *der Pilot* (pilot) _____
5. *das Mädchen* (girl) _____

Now change the indefinite article of each noun to the definite article. For example, when presented with *ein Vater*, you would say, *der Vater* to change it to the definite article. (Watch out! This one is trickier. Since masculine and neuter words both take the indefinite article *ein*, you'll have to recall the rules for determining gender in these cases.)

6. *ein Mantel* (coat) _____
7. *eine Lehrerin* (teacher) _____
8. *ein Kind* (child) _____
9. *ein Bruder* (brother) _____
10. *ein Richter* (judge) _____

Regular practice in choosing the correct gender of nouns will make the process much more comfortable over time. Making mistakes and using the wrong article is really quite common. Your accuracy will increase as you gain more experience. Keep trying, and gradually any problems with German gender will be a thing of the past.

CHAPTER 4

Forming Plurals and Using Pronouns

So you understand articles and that all nouns have gender. But what about when there are more than one of something? In the following sections, you'll learn how to talk about men, women, cars, books, and anything else you can have two or more of, plus you'll learn how to use pronouns so you don't have to keep repeating yourself.

Some Easy Plurals

Several German nouns are identical in the singular and the plural. You can tell when the noun is plural only by the verb used with it or by a number preceding it. Look at these examples:

ein Brunnen ist . . . (a well is . . .)
zehn Brunnen sind . . . (ten wells are . . .)

ein Mädchen ist . . . (a girl is . . .)
zehn Mädchen sind . . . (ten girls are . . .)

ein Schauspieler ist . . . (an actor is . . .)
zehn Schauspieler sind . . . (ten actors are . . .)

When a noun is plural, it uses *die* as its definite article, no matter what its gender. Very few German nouns form their plural by adding an *–s*, though a few do follow that pattern.

Singular Noun	Plural Noun
der Park (park)	*die Parks* (parks)
das Foto (photo)	*die Fotos* (photos)
die Kamera (camera)	*die Kameras* (cameras)

This is the simplest way that plurals may be formed, but it is not the typical way. Most plurals are formed in other ways, similar to irregular plurals in English, such as child/children, mouse/mice, and goose/geese.

The Plural of Masculine Nouns

Masculine nouns that end in *–er*, *–el*, or *–en* have no ending in the plural, but they may require adding an umlaut. Some examples with masculine nouns are shown in the following table.

▼ PLURAL OF MASCULINE NOUNS ENDING IN *–ER*, *–EL*, OR *–EN*

Singular Noun	Plural Noun with Numbers	Plural Noun with Definite Article
der Schauspieler (the actor)	*sechs Schauspieler* (six actors)	*die Schauspieler* (the actors)
der Löffel (the spoon)	*zwei Löffel* (two spoons)	*die Löffel* (the spoons)
der Laden (the shop)	*acht Läden* (eight shops)	*die Läden* (the shops)
der Vater (the father)	*drei Väter* (three fathers)	*die Väter* (the fathers)

Note how *Laden* and *Vater* have added an umlaut above the *a* in the plural form. Other masculine nouns, particularly short, one-syllable nouns, usually form their plural by adding *–e* to the noun. An umlaut is often required.

▼ MASCULINE PLURAL ENDING *–E*

Singular Noun	Plural Noun with Numbers	Plural Noun with Definite Article
der Abend (the evening)	*zwei Abende* (two evenings)	*die Abende* (the evenings)

Singular Noun	Plural Noun with Numbers	Plural Noun with Definite Article
der Arzt (the physician)	neun Ärzte (nine physicians)	die Ärzte (the physicians)
der Bahnhof (the train station)	zwei Bahnhöfe (two train stations)	die Bahnhöfe (the train stations)
der Brief (the letter)	sechs Briefe (six letters)	die Briefe (the letters)
der Bus (the bus)	zwei Busse (two buses)	die Busse (the buses)
der Freund (the friend)	sieben Freunde (seven friends)	die Freunde (the friends)
der Markt (the market)	drei Märkte (three markets)	die Märkte (the markets)
der Platz (the square)	zwei Plätze (two squares)	die Plätze (the squares)
der Roman (the novel)	fünf Romane (five novels)	die Romane (the novels)
der Sohn (the son)	vier Söhne (four sons)	die Söhne (the sons)
der Stuhl (the chair)	vier Stühle (four chairs)	die Stühle (the chairs)
der Tag (the day)	zehn Tage (ten days)	die Tage (the days)
der Zug (the train)	acht Züge (eight trains)	die Züge (the trains)

One high-frequency masculine noun that doesn't follow these patterns is *der Mann* (man). It forms its plural by adding an umlaut and the ending *–er*: *zwei Männer* (two men), *die Männer* (the men).

The Plural of Feminine Nouns

Just like masculine nouns, feminine nouns don't change to the plural simply by adding an *–s*. Most feminine nouns change to the plural by adding *–n* or *–en*. And just like all other plural nouns, they use *die* as the definite article.

▼ FORMING PLURALS OF FEMININE NOUNS BY ADDING *–N* OR *–EN*

Singular	Plural
die Frau (the woman)	die Frauen (the women)
die Schwester (the sister)	die Schwestern (the sisters)
die Straße (the street)	die Straßen (the streets)
die Tasse (the cup)	die Tassen (the cups)

If a feminine noun ends in *–in*, the plural ending is *–nen. Die Freundin* (girlfriend) becomes *die Freundinnen* (girlfriends).

There are two notable exceptions to the rule regarding *–n* or *–en* for feminine nouns. Note that the only change in these two words is the addition of an umlaut in the plural:

die Mutter (mother)	*die Mütter* (mothers)
die Tochter (daughter)	*die Töchter* (daughters)

The Plural of Neuter Nouns

Many neuter words follow a similar pattern to some masculine words: There is no ending change in the plural.

▼ NEUTER PLURAL FORMATION FOR NOUNS THAT TAKE NO ENDING

Singular	Plural
das Fenster (the window)	*die Fenster* (the windows)
das Klassenzimmer (the classroom)	*die Klassenzimmer* (the classrooms)
das Mädchen (the girl)	*die Mädchen* (the girls)

Neuter words, particularly those of one syllable, tend to form their plural by the ending *–er.* An umlaut may also be added in some cases.

▼ NEUTER PLURAL FORMATION FOR NOUNS THAT TAKE AN *–ER* ENDING

Singular	Plural
das Fahrrad (the bicycle)	*die Fahrräder* (the bicycles)
das Glas (the glass)	*die Gläser* (the glasses)
das Haus (the house)	*die Häuser* (the houses)
das Kind (the child)	*die Kinder* (the children)
das Land (the country)	*die Länder* (the countries)

Words that end in *–chen* and *–lein* change the article from *das* to *die*; no endings are added. *Das Mädchen* (the girl) becomes *die Mädchen* (the girls).

Be aware that these rules regarding plural formations only outline tendencies; they are meant to help guide you. There will always be exceptions. Using German plurals accurately will come with experience and time.

There is no indefinite article for the plural. Instead, just like English plural nouns, German plural nouns require no article when they represent a general plural noun.

die Schauspieler (the actors)   *Schauspieler* (actors)
die Mädchen (the girls)   *Mädchen* (girls)
die Freundinnen (the girlfriends)   *Freundinnen* (girlfriends)

Exercise 4-1

Change each of the following words to the plural.

1. *der Apfel* (apple) _____
2. *die Blume* (flower) _____
3. *das Buch* (book) _____
4. *der Garten* (garden) _____
5. *die Stunde* (hour) _____

He, She, and It

Now that you have a feeling for German gender, it's time to meet the pronouns that go along with the gender of nouns. Pronouns are words that take the place of a noun. They follow the patterns you have already learned with nouns. Interestingly, the German pronouns for "he," "she," and "it" closely resemble the definite articles.

▼ **THIRD PERSON SINGULAR PRONOUNS**

Gender	Definite Article	Pronoun
masculine	*der*	*er* (he or it)
feminine	*die*	*sie* (she or it)
neuter	*das*	*es* (he, she, or it)

Remember that German gender is not based on sexual gender. That's why *er* means both "he" and "it," and *sie* means both "she" and "it." It depends on the meaning of the noun. Look at these examples.

▼ PRONOUN SUBSTITUTION

Noun Subject	Pronoun Replacement	Translation
Der Mann ist da.	Er ist da.	He is there.
Der Mantel ist da.	Er ist da.	It is there.
Die Studentin ist in der Stadt.	Sie ist in der Stadt.	She is in the city.
Die Schule ist in der Stadt.	Sie ist in der Stadt.	It is in the city.
Das Kind ist hier.	Es ist hier.	He (or she) is here.
Das Geschenk ist hier.	Es ist hier.	It is here.

You and I

In addition to the third person pronouns that you just learned, you should know the first and second person personal pronouns.

▼ PERSONAL PRONOUNS—SINGULAR

Person	English Pronoun	German Pronoun
First	I	ich
Second	you	du (informal), Sie (formal)
Third	he, she, it	er, sie, es

Sie is the formal way to say "you," which you would use when addressing anyone you don't know or anyone who is older than you or in a position of authority. There's no exact English equivalent. It is always capitalized. And don't let the word for "she" or "it" (*sie*) confuse you, even though it looks the same—it's always spelled with a lowercase letter except at the beginning of a sentence.

The German word for the pronoun "I" is *ich* and is never capitalized, except at the beginning of a sentence.

Plural Pronouns

To talk about nouns that are plural without repeating them over and over, you'll need to use the plural pronouns.

▼ **PERSONAL PRONOUNS—PLURAL**

Person	English Pronoun	German Pronoun
First	we	*wir*
Second	you all or plural you	*ihr*
Third	they	*sie*

Here are some examples:

Vater und Mutter becomes *sie* (pl.)
Benno und Ilse becomes *sie* (pl.)
Karl und ich becomes *wir*
der Schüler und ich becomes *wir*

Using *du, ihr,* and *Sie*

German has three different pronouns that mean "you," as you have now seen. German has a plural, informal pronoun (the plural of *du*). It is *ihr.* Yes, it also means "you." And, of course, you've already encountered *Sie,* which is the formal pronoun "you." So let's look at those forms of "you" again and put them in perspective.

du (you, sing.)
Used to address one person on an informal or familiar basis

ihr (you, pl.)
Used to address more than one person on an informal or familiar basis

Sie (you, sing. or pl.)
Used to address one or more persons on a formal basis

"Informal" here means that the person to whom you are speaking is a relative, a close friend, or a younger person and you are on a first-name basis with one another. "Formal" here means that the person to whom you are speaking is older, in a position of respect or authority, or is someone you don't know well. You use a title and a last name when addressing this person: *Herr Braun, Professor Brenner, Frau Doktor Schmidt.*

Exercise 4-2

Fill in the blanks with the correct pronoun substitute for the subjects in parentheses.

1. _____ (*Maria*) *ist in der Schule.* (She is at the school.)
2. *Sind* _____ (*Karl und Luise*) *hier?* (Are they here?)
3. _____ (*der Diplomat*) *ist in Deutschland.* (He is in Germany.)
4. _____ (*Martin und ich*) *sind Amerikaner.* (We are Americans.)
5. *Wo ist* _____ (*die Schule*)? (Where is it?)

Describe That Noun!

Just like English adjectives, German adjectives can stand alone at the end of a phrase to describe a noun in a sentence. These adjectives are called predicate adjectives.

Das Kind ist klein.	The child is little.
Onkel Hans ist jung.	Uncle Hans is young.
Großmutter wird wütend.	Grandmother is getting furious.

In this regard, German and English adjectives are used in the very same way. But when an adjective stands directly in front of a noun, that's where English and German differ. German adjectives add an ending when they stand in front of a noun.

The little child is sad.	*Das kleine Kind ist traurig.*
The young man is playing soccer.	*Der junge Mann spielt Fußball.*
The old lady likes her.	*Die alte Dame hat sie gern.*

When using the definite article (*der, die, das*) with a singular noun, the adjective ending is –*e*. But if the noun is plural, the ending is –*en*.

Das kleine Kind ist traurig. Die kleinen Kinder sind traurig.
Der junge Mann spielt Fußball. Die jungen Männer spielen Fußball.
Die alte Dame hat sie gern. Die alten Damen haben sie gern.

▼ ADJECTIVES

German	English	German	English	German	English
arm	poor	hässlich	ugly	neu	new
blau	blue	hübsch	beautiful/handsome	reich	rich
braun	brown	interessant	interesting	rot	red
gelb	yellow	kurz	short	schwarz	black
grau	gray	lang	long	weiß	white
grün	green	langweilig	boring		

Here are some examples of predicate adjectives (which take no endings) compared to adjectives in front of the nouns they modify (which do take endings).

Die Lehrerin ist alt. (The teacher is old.)
die alte Lehrerin (the old teacher)
Das Kind ist klein. (The child is small.)
das kleine Kind (the small child)
Die Kinder sind traurig. (The children are sad.)
die traurigen Kinder (the sad children)
Die Frauen sind hübsch. (The women are beautiful.)
die hübschen Frauen (the beautiful women)
Die Vase ist grün. (The vase is green.)
die grüne Vase (the green vase)

Exercise 4-3

Fill in each blank with one of the colors listed here: *blau, braun, gelb, grau,* or *rot.*

1. *Die neue Vase ist* _____.
2. *Der alte BMW ist* _____.
3. *Die Rose ist* _____.
4. *Der neue Mantel ist* _____.
5. *Das Haus ist* _____.

CHAPTER 5

Using Verbs

A verb is one of the most important elements of any language. Verbs tell what's going on: singing, running, fighting, crying, sleeping, drinking, talking, loving, and on and on. In this chapter you'll learn how to conjugate verbs and form sentences. Before long, you'll be speaking like a native!

Conjugate What?

Infinitives are the basic form of verbs in any language. In English, infinitives begin with the word "to" and look like this: to run, to jump, to follow, to argue, to be. In German they end in *–n* or *–en: sein, gehen, heißen*.

Conjugating a verb means to put the appropriate endings on the verb that correspond to the various pronouns. In English that's a relatively simple matter. You drop the word "to" from the infinitive and add an *–s* to the third person singular (he, she, it).

▼ **VERB ENDINGS IN ENGLISH**

	to run	to speak	to be	to understand
I	run	speak	am	understand
you	run	speak	are	understand
he, she, it	runs	speaks	is	understands
we	run	speak	are	understand
they	run	speak	are	understand

When it comes to verbs, English is a little more complicated than German. Watch out for the two present tense forms that we have in English. German has only one. And both English forms are translated into German the same way. Look at these examples:

Ich kaufe ein Haus.	I buy a house.
Ich kaufe ein Haus.	I am buying a house.
Er geht nach Hause.	He goes home.
Er geht nach Hause.	He is going home.

The German Verb *sein*

You have already learned one of the most important verbs in German: *sein*. That's the infinitive form of the verb "to be."

▼ CONJUGATING *SEIN* (TO BE)

Person	English Conjugation	German Conjugation
First (sing.)	I am	*ich bin*
Second (sing.)	you are	*du bist, Sie sind*
Third (sing.)	he is, she is, it is	*er ist, sie ist, es ist*
First (pl.)	we are	*wir sind*
Second (pl.)	you are	*ihr seid*
Third (pl.)	they are	*sie sind*

Exercise 5-1

Fill in each blank with the appropriate form of *sein*.

1. *Ich* _____ *in Berlin.* (I am in Berlin.)
2. *Er* _____ *in Hamburg.* (He is in Hamburg.)
3. *Wir* _____ *in Deutschland.* (We are in Germany.)
4. *Du* _____ *in Amerika.* (You are in America.)
5. *Karl* _____ *in Frankfurt.* (Karl is in Frankfurt.)

Sie, sie, or sie?

There are three pronouns in German that look an awfully lot alike: *sie* (she), *Sie* (you formal), and *sie* (they). Germans have no problem distinguishing these pronouns, because their usage is so specific. For one thing, *sie ist* can mean only "she is," because the verb *ist* is used only with *er*, *sie* (she), and *es*. And the context of a conversation would make clear whether *Sie* (you formal) or *sie* (they) is meant.

 Question

> **How do I know which form of *sein* to use with names and nouns?**
> All names and nouns are third person singular or plural, which means they use *ist* if singular and *sind* if plural. For example: *Frau Keller ist in Mannheim.* (Ms. Keller [singular] is in Mannheim.) *Die Jungen sind in Bonn.* (The boys [plural] are in Bonn.)

In this book, you will know that "you" is the meaning of *Sie* when you see it with a capitalized *S*. The other two forms will be identified as singular and plural. If you see *sie* (sing.), you will know that it means "she." If you see *sie* (pl.), you will know it means "they."

Today

Heute (HOI-teh) means "today" and indicates that something is probably taking place in the present tense. It's an adverb that tells when something is occurring. When you use the verb *sein* in a sentence, you can add *heute* to indicate the present tense.

Er ist heute in Berlin.	He is in Berlin today.
Heute sind Sie in der Stadt.	Today you are in the city.

Here's an important rule: When something other than the subject starts a sentence, the verb comes before the subject. The verb should always go in the second position of a sentence, whether the sentence begins with a subject, adverb, or something else. For example, the sentence *Peter ist heute in Hamburg* (Peter is in Hamburg today) can be rephrased to emphasize the word *heute* by placing it first and inverting the subject and verb: *Heute ist Peter in Hamburg.*

Exercise 5-2

Practice conjugating the verb *sein* by filling in the appropriate form in the blank.

1. *Karl* _____ *in der Stadt.*
2. *Wir* _____ *in Schweden.*
3. *Ihr* _____ *in der Schule.*
4. *Du* _____ *in Freiburg.*
5. *Sie* (pl.) _____ *in den Alpen.*
6. *Petra* _____ *nicht da.*
7. *Ich* _____ *in Heidelberg.*
8. *Sie* (sing.) _____ *krank.*
9. *Frau Brenner* _____ *in Hamburg.*
10. *Sie* (pl.) _____ *in Deutschland.*

Verbs of Motion: Coming and Going

Let's look at four verbs that are called verbs of motion. They describe how you get from one place to another: *gehen* (GAY-en), to go on foot; *kommen* (KAW-men), to come; *fliegen* (FLEE-gen), to fly; and *fahren* (FAHR-en), to drive or to go by transportation.

These verbs are used almost in the same way that their English counterparts are used, except that German tends to be a little more specific. In English we say, "I go to school." We don't say whether we walk there, drive there, or fly there. In German there's a tendency to specify the means of conveyance: walking, driving, or flying. To learn how to conjugate these verbs, you need to know the term "verb stem." A verb stem is the part of the infinitive remaining when you drop the final –*en*: *fahren/fahr, gehen/ geh*, and so on. You add endings to the verb stem to conjugate each verb according to the person and number (singular or plural).

▼ CONJUGATIONAL ENDINGS OF VERBS

Person	Ending to Add to Verb Stem	Example
First (sing.)	*–e*	*ich gehe*
Second (sing.)	*–st*	*du gehst*
Third (sing.)	*–t*	*er, sie, es geht*
First (pl.)	*–en*	*wir gehen*
Second (pl.)	*–t*	*ihr geht*
Second formal (sing. or pl.)	*–en*	*Sie gehen*
Third (pl.)	*–en*	*sie gehen*

Now let's look at the conjugations of these verbs of motion.

▼ CONJUGATING VERBS OF MOTION

gehen	*kommen*	*fliegen*	*fahren*
ich gehe	*ich komme*	*ich fliege*	*ich fahre*
du gehst	*du kommst*	*du fliegst*	*du fährst*
er/sie/es geht	*er/sie/es kommt*	*er/sie/es fliegt*	*er/sie/es fährt*
wir gehen	*wir kommen*	*wir fliegen*	*wir fahren*
ihr geht	*ihr kommt*	*ihr fliegt*	*ihr fahrt*
Sie gehen	*Sie kommen*	*Sie fliegen*	*Sie fahren*
sie (pl.) gehen	*sie kommen*	*sie fliegen*	*sie fahren*

Notice that the second person singular and third person singular (*du, er, sie, es*) add an umlaut in their conjugation of the verb *fahren*: *du fährst, er fährt, sie fährt, es fährt*. This is called a stem change. Some other verbs also do this, but they will be addressed later.

 Fact

With feminine nouns use *in die* . . . to say that you're going to or into some place: *in die Stadt*. With neuter nouns use *ins* . . . (the contraction of *in das*) to say that you're going to some place: *ins Kino*. With masculine nouns you use in *den* . . . in *den Park* (into the park).

Let's look at some examples of ways to use these verbs.

Ihr kommt aus Berlin.	You all come from Berlin.
Wir fliegen nach Hause.	We fly home.
Er fährt mit dem Bus.	He goes (drives) by bus.
Ich gehe mit Hans.	I go with Hans.
Sie fahren mit dem Zug.	They are going by train.

The phrase *kommen aus* is used regularly to tell what city, locale, or country you come from: *Ich komme aus Hamburg. Er kommt aus Bayern* (Bavaria). *Wir kommen aus Amerika.*

Essentials for Life: Eating and Drinking

Essen (ESS-en) (to eat) and *trinken* (TRINK-en) (to drink) are not verbs of motion. But notice that their conjugation follows the same pattern as the other verbs you have learned. Take note that the verb *essen*, like *fahren*, requires a slight change in the second and third person singular *(du, er, sie, es)*: *du isst, er isst, sie isst, es isst.*

▼ CONJUGATING *ESSEN* AND *TRINKEN*

essen		trinken	
ich esse	*ihr esst*	*ich trinke*	*ihr trinkt*
du isst	*Sie essen*	*du trinkst*	*Sie trinken*
er/sie/es isst	*sie* (pl.) *essen*	*er/sie/es trinkt*	*sie trinken*
wir essen		*wir trinken*	

Other Useful Verbs

Now it's time to start collecting some useful ones to add to your vocabulary. This list includes words you'll need when shopping, seeking information, or carrying on a casual conversation.

▼ **PRESENT TENSE CONJUGATIONS OF SOME NEW VERBS**

German Infinitive	*ich*	*du*	*er/sie/es*	*wir*	*ihr*	*Sie/sie (pl.)*
lachen (to laugh)	*lache*	*lachst*	*lacht*	*lachen*	*lacht*	*lachen*
leben (to live)	*lebe*	*lebst*	*lebt*	*leben*	*lebt*	*leben*
wohnen (to live/ reside)	*wohne*	*wohnst*	*wohnt*	*wohnen*	*wohnt*	*wohnen*
lieben (to love)	*liebe*	*liebst*	*liebt*	*lieben*	*liebt*	*lieben*
brauchen (to need)	*brauche*	*brauchst*	*braucht*	*brauchen*	*braucht*	*brauchen*
spielen (to play)	*spiele*	*spielst*	*spielt*	*spielen*	*spielt*	*spielen*
sagen (to say)	*sage*	*sagst*	*sagt*	*sagen*	*sagt*	*sagen*
suchen (to seek)	*suche*	*suchst*	*sucht*	*suchen*	*sucht*	*suchen*
denken (to think)	*denke*	*denkst*	*denkt*	*denken*	*denkt*	*denken*
besuchen (to visit)	*besuche*	*besuchst*	*besucht*	*besuchen*	*besucht*	*besuchen*

Watch out for *leben* and *wohnen*. The former means "to live, to be alive." The latter means "to live or reside" somewhere. *Andreas lebt wie ein König.* (Andreas lives like a king.) *Andreas wohnt jetzt in Berlin.* (Andreas is living in Berlin now.)

The following are five more new verbs to add to your German vocabulary, but they have a variation in the verb stem that you'll have to watch for. If a German verb stem ends in *–d* or *–t*, you have to add an extra *–e* before adding a *–t* or an *–st* ending. This makes the conjugated verb easier to pronounce. You'll remember that the *–t* ending is needed after *er*, *sie*, *es*, and *ihr*, and *–st* is used after *du*.

German infinitive	ich	du	er/sie/es	wir	ihr	Sie/sie (pl.)
antworten (to answer)	antworte	antwortest	antwortet	antworten	antwortet	antworten
finden (to find)	finde	findest	findet	finden	findet	finden
senden (to send)	sende	sendest	sendet	senden	sendet	senden
warten (to wait)	warte	wartest	wartet	warten	wartet	warten
arbeiten (to work)	arbeite	arbeitest	arbeitet	arbeiten	arbeitet	arbeiten

Verbs That End in –ieren

There are numerous patterns of words that help to build a vocabulary rapidly. Another pattern is the verb ending –ieren. Verbs that have this ending tend to be very similar to English. And they're all regular verbs, so they don't require a change to the stem in conjugations. Here are useful words to learn:

akzeptieren (to accept)

arrangieren (to arrange)

diskutieren (to discuss)

isolieren (to isolate)

konfiszieren (to confiscate)

kontrollieren (to control, supervise)

kritisieren (to criticize)

marschieren (to march)

fotografieren (to photograph)

reduzieren (to reduce)

reparieren (to repair)

reservieren (to reserve)

riskieren (to risk)

studieren (to study)

Bitten: A Very Versatile Verb

The word bitten is one of the most frequently used German words. It has more than just one meaning, of course. Bitten means "to ask, to request" or "to beg." But it doesn't have anything to do with asking questions. It refers to asking someone to do something: "He asks her to remove her hat." "The teacher asks the class to remain very quiet."

Er bittet sie, mitzukommen.	He asks them to come along.
Ich bitte ihn, nach Hause zu kommen.	I ask him to come home.

In addition, you will often hear the word when you walk up to a salesperson in a store. *Bitte*, the salesperson will say cheerfully. Or, *Bitte schön*. It's comparable to "May I help you?" in English. When the salesperson hands you your purchase, he or she might also say, *Bitte schön*. In this case it means something like "Here you are," or "Here's your package." And when you thank the salesperson (*danke schön*), the response will be *bitte schön* or *bitte sehr* (you're welcome).

And, finally, the word *bitte* is also used just like our word "please." It's a little word, but it's used in so many interesting ways.

Gehen Sie bitte ins Wohnzimmer!	Go into the living room, please.
Der nächste bitte!	Next, please.
Nehmen Sie bitte Platz!	Please take a seat.

Du Versus Sie Again

Germans use the informal pronoun *du* and the formal pronoun *Sie* with great care. There are unspoken rules that you must learn to follow.

When speaking to children, be assured that you can always address them with *du*. Among themselves, even with new children in their group, children always use *du*. There is a verb for this. Its infinitive is *duzen* (DOOTZ-en) and means to say *du* and to be on an informal or familiar basis. People who use this form say *Wir duzen einander.* (We use *du* with one another.)

Siezen (ZEETZ-en) is the infinitive that means that you are on a formal basis. Use *Sie* in all cases with adult strangers: the receptionist at an office, a clerk in a store, a teacher, etc. Once you get to know someone well, you can suggest that you "officially" stop *siezen* and begin *duzen*. You remind one another what your first names are, and from then on you address one another by your first names and with the pronoun *du*. Some people still go through a little ceremony—usually over a glass of beer or wine—before commencing *duzen*. They lock arms and drink to *Freundschaft* (friendship).

Although these formalities still exist in German culture, many young people consider them old-fashioned and try to avoid the formal *Sie*.

Negation with "Not" and "Not Any"

To negate a sentence in German, you can use the words *nicht* (not) or *kein* (not any). The word *nicht* comes after the verb. However, if you have a sentence that uses the indefinite article *ein*, you can't use *nicht*. To negate *ein*, you use the word *kein* (KINE), which means "not any" or "no." *Kein* always replaces *ein*.

Ich bin nicht Peter.	I am not Peter.
Er wohnt nicht in München.	He does not live in Munich.
Sie studiert nicht Französisch.	She is not studying French.
Ich habe kein Geld.	I don't have any money.
Ich habe keinen Teller.	I have no plate.

The same endings you learned to use with *ein* must also be used with *kein*. You'll learn more about the endings that *ein* words can take in the next chapter.

▼ NEGATING *EIN* IN THE GENDERS

Masculine	Feminine	Neuter	English Meaning
kein	*keine*	*kein*	not a/not any

Sie sehen eine Brücke. Sie sehen keine Brücke.
Ich kaufe einen Teller. Ich kaufe keinen Teller.

Let's look at some other negative words. You already know words like *nein*, *nicht*, and *kein*. Using them as a foundation, you can discover myriad negative words that will greatly enrich your vocabulary.

▼ WORDS DERIVED FROM NEGATIVES

German	English Meaning
keinerlei	not any
keinesfalls	on no account
keineswegs	by no means
nichts	nothing
nichtsdestoweniger	nonetheless
nie	never
niemals	never
niemand	no one
Niemandsland	no man's land
nirgendwo	nowhere
weder . . . noch	neither . . . nor

Exercise 5-3

Practice conjugating verbs by filling in the correct form of the verb given in parentheses.

1. *Sie (gehen)* _____ *in die Metzgerei.* (She goes to the butcher shop.)
2. *Sie (fahren)* _____ *ins Kino.* (She goes [drives] to the movies.)
3. *Ich (kaufen)* _____ *einen Bleistift.* (I buy a pencil.)
4. *Sie (trinken)* _____ *kein Bier.* (She doesn't drink beer.)
5. *Herr Martini (kommen)* _____ *aus Italien.* (Mr. Martini comes from Italy.)

CHAPTER 6

Verbs with Quirks

Now that you've learned the basics about German verbs, it's time to look more closely at some verbs that take stem changes in the present tense. One of the most often used is the verb "to have." This chapter will also cover using the present tense to talk about the future and introduce you to verbs that take prefixes.

The German Verb *haben*

One very common German verb is "to have"—*haben*. This verb doesn't follow the rules of conjugation exactly. In the second and third person singular, the stem of the verb (the part left after you drop the *–en*) changes. It's time to become acquainted with the little irregularities found in this verb.

▼ CONJUGATING *HABEN* (TO HAVE)

Person	English Conjugation	German Conjugation
First (sing.)	I have	*ich habe*
Second (sing.)	you have	*du hast*
Third (sing.)	he/she/it has	*er/sie/es hat*
First (pl.)	we have	*wir haben*
Second (pl.)	you all have	*ihr habt*
Second (formal)	you have	*Sie haben*
Third (pl.)	they have	*sie* (pl.) *haben*

Practice saying the conjugation of the verb and memorize it. It's a very important verb to know. And just like *sein*, you can use it in a sentence with *heute* to indicate the present tense.

Maria hat ein Examen.	Maria has an exam.
Heute haben wir eine Übung.	We are having an exercise today.
Ich habe eine Klasse.	I have a class.
Du hast es.	You have it.
Er hat eine Prüfung.	He has a test.

Expressing Affection with *haben*

German has a special way of saying that a person likes someone. To express "like" in German, conjugate *haben*, say whom it is you like, and follow the whole phrase with the word *gern*.

▼ USING *GERN HABEN* TO EXPRESS LIKE

Conjugate haben	Direct Object (whom you like)	*gern*	English Meaning
Ich habe	*Peter*	*gern.*	I like Peter.
Du hast	*das Mädchen*	*gern.*	You like the girl.
Wir haben	*sie*	*gern.*	We like them.
Haben Sie	*Karl oder Hans*	*gern?*	Do you like Karl or Hans?

You can also use *gern* following other verbs to show that you like doing something:

Ich esse gern Obst.	I like eating fruit.
Er trinkt gern Bier.	He likes drinking beer.
Wir singen gern.	We like singing.

This is a very common phrase and one to add to your vocabulary.

The Word *morgen*

Morgen means "tomorrow" and indicates that something is occurring in the future. It is an adverb that tells when something will occur. But you can use the present tense of a verb and still mean the future. It's just like English. You can specify the time by mentioning "today" or "tomorrow" using only a present tense verb.

Today he is in Germany.
Tomorrow he is in Germany.
He has a class today.
He has a class tomorrow.

Look at these examples:

Heute sind wir in Hamburg.	We are in Hamburg today.
Morgen sind wir in Hamburg.	We are in Hamburg tomorrow.
Heute habe ich eine Prüfung.	I have a test today.
Morgen habe ich eine Prüfung.	I have a test tomorrow.

You can also use the present tense to infer a future meaning using verbs of motion.

Heute kommt er ins Kino.	He is coming to the movies today.
Morgen kommt er ins Kino.	He is coming to the movies tomorrow.
Heute fliegen wir nach Hause.	We are flying home today.
Morgen fliegen wir nach Hause.	We are flying home tomorrow.

Exercise 6-1

Restate each sentence in the future tense by starting with the word *morgen*. (Don't forget that the verb must remain in the second position. You'll need to invert the subject and verb in your new sentence.)

1. *Er geht ins Kino.* (He is going to the movies.)

2. *Sie* (pl.) *fliegen nach Hause.* (They are flying home.)

---

3. *Ich gehe ins Museum.* (I am going to the museum.)

---

4. *Ludwig kommt nicht ins Restaurant.* (Ludwig is not coming to the restaurant.)

---

5. *Du fährst in die Stadt.* (You drive in the city.)

Stem Changes in the Present Tense

You learned earlier that German has some special forms in the present tense of certain verbs. The verb *fahren*, for example, requires an umlaut in the second person singular (*du*) and third person singular (*er, sie, es*): *ich fahre, du fährst, er fährt*, etc.

Three other verbs you should know also need special changes. But notice that each verb has its own unique way of changing. The verb *wissen* (to know) becomes a new form, the verb *sprechen* (to speak) changes the vowel *e* to *i*, and the verb *laufen* (to run) adds an umlaut. When a pair of vowels that can both take the umlaut appear together, the umlaut is always added to the first vowel—as in the case of *laufen* (*-äu-*).

▼ THE CONJUGATION OF *WISSEN, SPRECHEN,* AND *LAUFEN*

Pronoun	wissen	sprechen	laufen
ich	*weiß*	*spreche*	*laufe*
du	*weißt*	*sprichst*	*läufst*
er, sie, es	*weiß*	*spricht*	*läuft*
wir	*wissen*	*sprechen*	*laufen*
ihr	*wisst*	*sprecht*	*lauft*
Sie, sie (pl.)	*wissen*	*sprechen*	*laufen*

Be careful of the spelling of the conjugation of *wissen*. There is no ending on the stem of the verb *weiß* with the pronouns *ich, er, sie*, and *es*. And with the pronoun *du* you only add a *–t* to the stem *weiß* (*du weißt*).

There aren't many verbs that change their form the way *wissen* does. But there are lots of useful words that follow the patterns of *sprechen* and *laufen*. Many words that have an *e* in the verb stem, like *sprechen*, change that *e* to an *i* or *ie*. And words that have the vowel *a* in the stem often add an umlaut, like *laufen*. But remember that these little changes only occur in the second person singular (*du*) and the third person singular (*er, sie, es*). Here are some examples.

▼ VERBS THAT CHANGE *E* TO *I*

English	German Infinitive	Conjugation with *ich*, *du*, and *er*		
to break	*brechen*	*ich breche*	*du brichst*	*er bricht*
to give	*geben*	*ich gebe*	*du gibst*	*er gibt*
to help	*helfen*	*ich helfe*	*du hilfst*	*er hilft*
to meet	*treffen*	*ich treffe*	*du triffst*	*er trifft*
to take	*nehmen*	*ich nehme*	*du nimmst*	*er nimmt*

▼ VERBS THAT CHANGE *E* TO *IE*

English	German Infinitive	Conjugation with *ich*, *du*, and *er*		
to read	*lesen*	*ich lese*	*du liest*	*er liest*
to see	*sehen*	*ich sehe*	*du siehst*	*er sieht*

▼ VERBS THAT CHANGE *A* TO *Ä*

English	German Infinitive	Conjugation with *ich*, *du*, and *er*		
to bake	*backen*	*ich backe*	*du bäckst*	*er bäckt**
to sleep	*schlafen*	*ich schlafe*	*du schläfst*	*er schläft*
to fall	*fallen*	*ich falle*	*du fällst*	*er fällt*
to carry, wear	*tragen*	*ich trage*	*du trägst*	*er trägt*
to wash	*waschen*	*ich wasche*	*du wäschst*	*er wäscht*
to let	*lassen*	*ich lasse*	*du lässt*	*er lässt*
to catch	*fangen*	*ich fange*	*du fängst*	*er fängt*

*Both *er bäckt* and *er backt* are acceptable present tense forms.

Exercise 6-2

In the sentences below, fill in the correct form of the verb in parentheses.

1. *Das Kind* _____ *(sprechen) kein Deutsch.* (The child doesn't speak German.)
2. *Du* _____ *(schlafe) im Wohnzimmer.* (You sleep in the living room.)
3. *(Sehen)* _____ *du die Alpen?* (Do you see the Alps?)
4. *Peter* _____ *(helfen) Frau Meier.* (Peter helps Ms. Meier.)
5. *Vater* _____ *(treffen) meine Freundin.* (Father meets my girlfriend.)

The Many Uses of *werden*

Werden is a frequently used verb in German. It means "to become" or "to get." (She is becoming a doctor. It's getting warm.) Its conjugation follows the pattern you already know, with a slight variation in the second and third persons singular.

▼ CONJUGATING *WERDEN* (TO GET / TO BECOME)

Person	English Conjugation	German Conjugation
First (sing.)	I get / I become	*ich werde*
Second (sing.)	you get / you become	*du wirst*
Third (sing.)	he/she/it gets / he/she/it becomes	*er/sie/es wird*
First (pl.)	we get / we become	*wir werden*
Second (pl.)	you all get / you all become	*ihr werdet*
Second (formal)	you get / you become	*Sie werden*
Third (pl.)	they get / they become	*sie werden*

Jobs and Professions

Just as English speakers tell what they want to become in the future, Germans do the same thing by using the verb *werden*.

Meine Schwester wird Ärztin.	My sister is becoming a doctor.
Sie (pl.) *werden Schauspieler.*	They're becoming actors.
Wirst du Lehrling?	Are you becoming an apprentice?

When you speak about your dream or your wish for the future, you use the phrase *Ich möchte . . . werden* (I'd like to become a . . .). Careful: *Werden* must come at the end of the sentence in this usage.

Ich möchte Professor werden.	I'd like to become a professor.
Hans möchte Pilot werden.	Hans would like to become a pilot.
Was möchten Sie werden?	What would you like to become?
Wir möchten Sänger werden.	We would like to become singers.

Notice that the conjugational endings for *möchten* have a slight irregularity: *ich möchte, du möchtest, er möchte, wir möchten, ihr möchtet, Sie möchten, sie möchten.*

The same verb *werden*, conjugated as *es wird*, is commonly used to tell that there is a change coming: It's getting cold. It's getting dark. It's getting noisy. And just like English, German usually blames it all on "it."

Es wird kalt.	It's getting cold.
Es wird heiß.	It's getting hot.
Es wird warm.	It's getting warm.
Es wird kühl.	It's getting cool.
Es wird dunkel.	It's getting dark.
Es wird hell.	It's getting bright.
Es wird laut.	It's getting loud. / It's getting noisy.
Es wird leise.	It's getting quiet.

Various nouns and pronouns can use this form of the verb, too: He's getting old. Are you getting sick? How old will you be?

Großvater wird alt.	Grandfather is getting old.
Werden Sie krank?	Are you getting sick?
Wie alt wirst du?	How old will you be?
Warum wird er rot?	Why is he getting (turning) red?

Sie wird sehr energisch.	She's getting very energetic.
Der Hund wird müde.	The dog's getting tired.
Großmutter wird wütend.	Grandmother's becoming furious.
Der Patient wird wieder stark.	The patient is getting strong again.

Having Respect for Prefixes

You have probably noticed by now that many German words appear with different prefixes. Those prefixes change the meaning of a word, but they don't change how the basic word functions. For example, an irregular verb is still irregular no matter what the prefix might be.

Take a look at what German prefixes can do to a verb.

▼ **PREFIXES WITH GERMAN WORDS**

Prefix	Basic Word	Meaning	Prefix Added	New Meaning
be–	*kommen*	to come	*bekommen*	to receive
an–	*kommen*	to come	*ankommen*	to arrive
er–	*schlagen*	to hit	*erschlagen*	to kill, strike dead
auf–	*schlagen*	to hit	*aufschlagen*	to open (a book)
bei–	*bringen*	to bring	*beibringen*	to teach
um–	*bringen*	to bring	*umbringen*	to murder

Inseparable Prefixes

The inseparable prefixes are just what the word "inseparable" implies: They cannot be separated from the verb. The inseparable prefixes are: *be–*, *ent–*, *emp–*, *er–*, *ge–*, *ver–*, and *zer–*. Here are some verbs that have these prefixes: *bekommen* (to receive, get), *entlassen* (to set free, dismiss), *empfinden* (to perceive), *erwarten* (to expect), *gehören* (to belong to), *verstehen* (to understand), and *zerbrechen* (to break to pieces). As you can see, these look similar to verbs you have already learned, but now they have a prefix on them. They are conjugated the same way, whether they have a prefix or not. That means that if they are regular verbs without a prefix, they are regular verbs with a prefix. Irregular verbs also remain irregular despite any prefix.

When these prefixes are attached to a word, the accent is always on the second syllable: *besuchen* (beh-ZOO**CH**-en) (to visit), *gebrauchen* (geh-BROW**CH**-en) (to use), *verlachen* (fair-LU**CH**-en) (to laugh at).

▼ **CONJUGATING VERBS WITH AND WITHOUT INSEPARABLE PREFIXES**

Verb with No Prefix	English Meaning	Verb with Inseparable Prefix	English Meaning
ich komme	I come	*ich bekomme*	I receive
er wartet	he waits	*er erwartet*	he expects
wir stehen	we stand	*wir verstehen*	we understand

Separable Prefixes

The separable prefixes are well named, because they are removed from the infinitive when the verb is conjugated in the present tense. Some of the primary separable prefixes are: *an, auf, aus, bei, ein, her, hin, mit, nach, um,* and *weg*. There are several others that act in the same way as the ones listed here. You'll encounter them as you gain more experience with German.

To conjugate a verb with a separable prefix, place the prefix at the end of the sentence and conjugate the verb normally. For example, the infinitive *ansehen* (to look at) in the present tense:

Ich sehe . . . an.   *Wir sehen . . . an.*
Du siehst . . . an.   *Ihr seht . . . an.*
Er sieht . . . an.   *Sie sehen . . . an.*

Take careful note of how prefixes change the meaning of these words:

hören (to hear)
gehören (to belong to)
aufhören (to stop, cease)
nehmen (to take)
benehmen (*sich*) (to behave [oneself])
annehmen (to assume)
stehen (to stand)

verstehen (to understand)

bestehen (aus) (to consist [of])

Be savvy about prefixes. Always check out the prefix of a word before assuming what the word means. Although you know *stehen* means "to stand," that information can't necessarily help you know what *entstehen* means. (By the way, *entstehen* means "to originate.") You know *nehmen* means "to take." But the meaning of the verb *er nimmt . . . an* and of the verb *er nimmt . . . ab* has been altered to "he assumes" and "he reduces." Never underestimate the importance of the prefix.

Let's take a look at how a variety of prefixes change the meaning of just one verb.

▼ *KOMMEN* AND PREFIXES

German Infinitive	English Meaning
kommen	to come
abkommen	to get away
ankommen	to arrive
auskommen	to make do
bekommen	to receive
einkommen	to come in
entkommen	to escape
herkommen	to come here
mitkommen	to come along
nachkommen	to come after
verkommen	to decay
vorkommen	to happen
zukommen	to approach

Using German well means knowing about prefixes and using them properly. Practice and experience will give you the skill to do just that. But don't be afraid to experiment or be creative. However, if you look for a specific word in a dictionary, read the fine print. It'll give you the information you need to select the right word for what you want to say.

Let's assume that you're looking for the German word for "to stir." Here are some of the vocabulary words you'll find: *erregen* (to stir, to stimulate, to excite), *anregen* (to stir, to incite, to suggest), *aufregen* (to stir, to rouse, to irritate), *rühren* (to stir, to touch, to move). If it's a soup you want to stir, you're probably looking for *quirlen*.

Prefixes with Verbs of Motion

Let's look at how the same prefixes affect different verbs. Some verbs of motion are *gehen, fahren, fliegen, laufen,* and *reisen*. Certain prefixes can be used with them. Let's look at what happens.

▼ **PREFIXES WITH VERBS OF MOTION**

Prefix	gehen	fahren	fliegen	laufen	reisen
ab–	—	abfahren	abfliegen	ablaufen	abreisen
	—	depart	fly off	run down	depart
an–	angehen	anfahren	anfliegen	anlaufen	—
	approach	drive up to	fly to	run up to	—
aus–	ausgehen	ausfahren	ausfliegen	auslaufen	die Ausreise
	go out	take for a drive	leave home	flow out	journey abroad
durch–	durchgehen	durchfahren	durchfliegen	durchlaufen	durchreisen
	go through	drive through	fly through	run through	travel through
ein–	eingehen	—	einfliegen	einlaufen	die Einreise
	go in	—	test a plane	enter a harbor	entry into a country
ent–	entgehen	—	—	entlaufen	—
	get away from	—	—	run away	—
entlang–	entlanggehen	entlangfahren	entlangfliegen	entlanglaufen	—
	go alongside	drive alongside	fly alongside	run alongside	—

Prefix	gehen	fahren	fliegen	laufen	reisen
mit–	mitgehen	mitfahren	mitfliegen	mitlaufen	mitreisen
	go along	drive with	fly along	run with	travel with
um–	umgehen	umfahren	umfliegen	umlaufen	umreisen
	make a detour	run over	fly round	run down	travel round
ver–	vergehen	—	verfliegen	verlaufen	verreisen
	pass	—	fly away	elapse	go on a journey
weg–	weggehen	wegfahren	—	weglaufen	wegreisen
	go away	cart away	—	run away	set out on a journey

Exercise 6-3

Restate each verb with the pronouns *ich* and *er.* For example:

kommen	ich komme	er kommt
fahren		
mitkommen		
bekommen		
lesen		
verstehen		
sprechen		
beibringen		
fallen		
aufhören		
erwarten		

CHAPTER 7

Direct Objects and the Accusative Case

In the following sections, you will learn even more about German nouns. Not only will you learn how to use nouns as the direct objects of sentences, you'll also be introduced to a new case—the accusative case—and learn how this affects articles and adjective endings.

Direct Objects Aren't Scary at All

Don't let the term "direct object" fool you. It's not as mysterious as it sounds, and it's something you use in English every day of your life. To discover the direct object in a sentence, just ask "what" or "whom" with the verb.

▼ FINDING THE DIRECT OBJECT

Sentence	What or Whom?	Direct Object
John buys a car.	What does John buy?	car
She kisses the boy.	Whom does she kiss?	boy
I like it.	What do I like?	it
We visited them.	Whom did we visit?	them
She sent a long list of problems to the dean.	What did she send?	list

The English Direct Object

When we speak or write in English, we don't think about what word is a subject or a direct object. We automatically know what changes, if any, are needed as we use these forms.

English nouns as direct objects don't look any different from when they're used as subjects. But pronouns make a slight change. Take a look at these examples:

▼ NOUNS AND PRONOUNS AS DIRECT OBJECTS

Noun as Subject	Noun as Direct Object
The man is here.	John greets the man.
A letter came for you.	John is reading a letter.
Uncle Tom dropped by.	John doesn't know Uncle Tom.
Pronoun as Subject	**Pronoun as Direct Object**
I speak German.	John just met me.
He arrived yesterday.	John picked him up at noon.
We are foreigners.	John helps us.
They buy a car.	John didn't like them.

The German Direct Object

German is very similar to English in that some nouns—feminine and neuter nouns, specifically—don't change when they're used as direct objects. And just like English, most German pronouns do require changes. Look at these examples.

▼ GERMAN NOUNS AND PRONOUNS AS DIRECT OBJECTS

Noun as Subject	Noun as Direct Object
Die Schule ist in der Stadt. (The school is in the city.)	*Sie* (pl.) *sehen die Schule.* (They see the school.)
Die Lehrerin ist da. (The teacher is there.)	*Sie* (pl.) *sehen die Lehrerin.* (They see the teacher.)
Das Geschenk ist hier. (The gift is here.)	*Sie* (pl.) *sehen das Geschenk.* (They see the gift.)

Pronoun as Subject	Pronoun as Direct Object
Ich bin in Berlin. (I am in Berlin.)	*Sie* (pl.) *sehen mich.* (They see me.)
Du bist in Hamburg. (You are in Hamburg.)	*Sie* (pl.) *sehen dich.* (They see you.)
Er heißt Hans. (His name is Hans.)	*Sie* (pl.) *sehen ihn.* (They see him.)
Sie heißt Anna. (Her name is Anna.)	*Sie* (pl.) *sehen sie.* (They see her.)
Es ist nicht da. (It is not there.)	*Sie* (pl.) *sehen es.* (They see it.)
Wir sind in Amerika. (We are in America.)	*Sie* (pl.) *sehen uns.* (They see us.)
Ihr seid in der Stadt. (You all are in the city.)	*Sie* (pl.) *sehen euch.* (They see you all.)
Sie heißen Thomas. (Your name is Thomas.)	*Sie* (pl.) *sehen Sie.* (They see you.)
Sie (pl.) *sind in Bonn.* (They are in Bonn.)	*Sie* (pl.) *sehen sie.* (They see them.)

Nominative and Accusative

Don't let those two words fool you. They're just fancy words that describe what you've just learned. The nominative case is the name given to the subject of a sentence. The subject is said to be in the nominative case.

English: The boy is going to the park.
German: *Der Junge geht zum Park.*

Direct objects are said to be in the accusative case.

English: My brother knows the teacher.
German: *Mein Bruder kennt den Lehrer.*

Whenever you change a masculine noun from *der Mann* to *den Mann*, you have changed it from the nominative to the accusative case. With feminine and neuter nouns, the nominative and accusative cases are identical. This is also true of plural nouns.

Mein Bruder kennt den Lehrer.	My brother knows the teacher.
Mein Bruder kennt die Lehrer.	My brother knows the teachers.

▼ **DEFINITE ARTICLES IN THE ACCUSATIVE CASE**

Masculine	Feminine	Neuter	Plural
den	die	das	die

Indefinite articles are similar. The indefinite articles for feminine and neuter nouns do not change when they are in the accusative case, but masculine indefinite articles require an –en ending.

▼ **INDEFINITE ARTICLES IN THE ACCUSATIVE CASE**

Masculine	Feminine	Neuter	Plural
einen	eine	ein	keine

A verb that is often followed by a direct object is *haben* (to have). Look at these examples.

Sie (pl.) *haben die Zeitung.*	They have the newspaper.
Wir haben ein Problem.	We have a problem.
Hans und Luise haben eine Zeitung.	Hans and Luise have a newspaper.
Sie (pl.) *haben ein Heft.*	They have a notebook.
Karl und Anna haben das Buch.	Karl and Anna have the book.
Haben Sie ein Auto?	Do you have a car?
Andreas und ich haben die Jacke.	Andreas and I have the jacket.

Let's look now at what the pronouns do when they appear as direct objects. Their form must also be changed into the accusative case.

▼ **PRONOUNS IN THE ACCUSATIVE CASE**

Person	Nominative Pronoun	Accusative Pronoun	English Meaning
First (sing.)	ich	mich	me
Second (sing.)	du	dich	you
Third (sing.)	er/sie/es	ihn/sie/es	him/her/it
First (pl.)	wir	uns	us
Second (pl.)	ihr	euch	you

Person	Nominative Pronoun	Accusative Pronoun	English Meaning
Second (formal)	*Sie*	*Sie*	you
Third (pl.)	*sie*	*sie*	them

Exercise 7-1

Practice using the accusative by changing the underlined noun direct object in each sentence to the appropriate pronoun direct object. For example, when presented with the sentence *Sie haben eine Zeitung*, you would change it to *Sie haben sie*.

1. *Sie haben die Bluse.* (They have the blouse.) _____
2. *Sie haben eine Jacke.* (They have a jacket.) _____
3. *Haben Sie die Zeitung?* (Do you have the newspaper?) _____
4. *Sehen Sie das Bett?* (Do you see the bed?) _____
5. *Hans und Andreas sehen den Lehrer nicht.*
   (Hans and Andreas do not see the teacher.) _____

Using Adjectives with Direct Objects

You know how to identify a direct object by asking "what" or "whom" with the verb in the sentence: He likes tea. What does he like? ("Tea" is the direct object.) He likes Mary. Whom does he like? ("Mary" is the direct object.)

This rule doesn't change when you add adjectives before the direct object: He likes hot tea. What does he like? ("Hot tea" is the direct object.) She likes the handsome German boy. Whom does she like? ("The handsome German boy" is the direct object.)

You learned that masculine nouns as direct objects change in the accusative case. That means that *der Mann* becomes *den Mann*. The same *–en* ending occurs when an adjective is added: *der alte Mann* becomes *den alten Mann* in the accusative case. Since the feminine and neuter are identical in both the nominative and accusative cases, there is no change in the adjective ending when they are used as direct objects. The accusative plural ending is *–en*.

Look at the pattern of adjective endings in the nominative and accusative cases.

▼ **COMPARING THE NOMINATIVE AND ACCUSATIVE CASES**

Case	Masculine	Feminine	Neuter	Plural
Nom.	der kleine Tisch	die kleine Flasche	das kleine Buch	die kleinen Bücher
Acc.	den kleinen Tisch	die kleine Flasche	das kleine Buch	die kleinen Bücher

Let's look at some examples using adjectives with direct objects:

Der neue Schüler wohnt in Deutschland.	The new student lives in Germany.
Wir besuchen den neuen Schüler.	We visit the new student.
Die arme Frau kommt aus Österreich.	The poor woman comes from Austria.
Hören Sie die arme Frau?	Do you hear the poor woman?

A few masculine nouns in the accusative case require an ending like the articles and adjectives that modify them. For example:

(Nom.) *der gute Junge*	(Acc.) *den guten Jungen* (the good boy)
(Nom.) *der alte Herr*	(Acc.) *den alten Herrn* (the old man)
(Nom.) *der hübsche Soldat*	(Acc.) *den hübschen Soldaten* (the handsome soldier)

Prepositions That Take the Accusative

The accusative case is also required after certain prepositions, such as *für* (for), *gegen* (against), and *ohne* (without). That means that if a noun is used as a direct object or if it follows one of those prepositions, it must be in the accusative case. Let's meet all of the prepositions that take the accusative case.

bis (to, till)   *um* (around, at)   *wider* (against)
ohne (without)   *für* (for)   *gegen* (against)
durch (through)

Be aware that *gegen* and *wider* have the same meaning: "against." But *wider* is rarely used in modern German.

▼ **ACCUSATIVE CASE WITH DIRECT OBJECTS AND PREPOSITIONS**

Gender	Direct Object	Preposition
Masculine	*Ich sehe den Mann.* (I see the man.)	*Es ist für den Mann.* (It is for the man.)
Feminine	*Ich sehe die Frau.* (I see the woman.)	*Es ist für die Frau.* (It is for the woman.)
Neuter	*Ich sehe das Kind.* (I see the child.)	*Es ist für das Kind.* (It is for the child.)
Plural	*Ich sehe die Kinder.* (I see the children.)	*Es ist für die Kinder.* (It is for the children.)

Pronouns work the same way.

▼ **ACCUSATIVE PRONOUNS WITH PREPOSITIONS**

Pronoun	As Direct Object	With Preposition
ich	*Sie sehen mich.* (They see me.)	*Es ist für mich.* (It's for me.)
du	*Sie sehen dich.* (They see you.)	*Es ist für dich.* (It's for you.)
er	*Sie sehen ihn.* (They see him.)	*Es ist für ihn.* (It's for him.)
sie (sing.)	*Sie sehen sie.* (They see her.)	*Es ist für sie.* (It's for her.)
wir	*Sie sehen uns.* (They see us.)	*Es ist für uns.* (It's for us.)
ihr	*Sie sehen euch.* (They see all of you.)	*Es ist für euch.* (It's for all of you.)
Sie (formal)	*Sie sehen Sie.* (They see you.)	*Es ist für Sie.* (It's for you.)
sie (pl.)	*Sie sehen sie.* (They see them.)	*Es ist für sie.* (It's for them.)

Let's take a look at all the accusative prepositions and how they're used.

bis: *Warte bis nächsten Montag!* (Wait until next Monday!)

bis: *Sie fahren bis Hamburg.* (They're driving to [as far as] Hamburg.)

durch: *Sie laufen durch den Garten.* (They run through the garden.)

durch: *Ich fahre durch Hannover.* (I'm driving through Hanover.)

für: *Das Geschenk ist für Karl.* (The gift is for Karl.)

gegen: *Er ist nicht gegen dich.* (He's not against you.)

ohne: *Sie kommt ohne Jens.* (She comes without Jens.)

ohne: *Sie geht ohne den Bruder ins Kino.* (She is going to the movies without her brother.)

um: *Sie fährt mit dem Wagen um den See.* (She drives around the lake by car.)

wider: *Wer nicht für uns ist, ist wider (gegen) uns.* (Whoever's not for us is against us.)

Exercise 7-2

Complete each sentence with the words provided in parentheses. For example:

(Berlin/Darmstadt) Sie fahren bis . . .
Sie fahren bis Berlin.
Sie fahren bis Darmstadt

1. *(Peter / meine Schwester) Die Jungen kommen ohne . . .*

   _____

   _____

2. *(das Schloss* [palace] */ die Kirche* [church]*) Wir fahren mit dem Wagen um . . .*

   _____

   _____

3. *(das Haus / der Bahnhof* [train station]*) Ich gehe durch . . .*

   _____

   _____

4. *(Frau Schneider / das Mädchen) Sie hat ein Buch für* . . .

_____

_____

5. *(mich/uns) Bist du gegen* . . . ?

_____

_____

Es gibt . . .

German has a strange little expression that literally makes no sense in English but is a valuable tool in German. It's *es gibt*, and the two words mean "it gives."

But that's just the literal translation. *Es gibt* is an important idiom that translates into English as "there is" or "there are." Think about it in English, first: "There's a bug on the wall!" "There were several foreigners among the guests."

In most cases you can use *es gibt* in place of "there is / there are" and you won't go wrong. But be careful! The word or phrase that follows *es gibt* has to be in the accusative case. Once again, that means you have to watch out for masculine nouns, which make a change in that case.

Let's look at some examples.

Heute mittag gibt es Gulaschsuppe.
There's goulash for lunch today.

Gibt es viele Bücher in deiner Bibliothek?
Are there a lot of books in your library?

Heute zum Abendessen gibt es keinen Wein.
There's no wine at supper today.

Other Useful Idioms

Did you know that German has slang and idiomatic expressions just like English?

Imagine a person who's just learning English hears someone say, "Get a load of her!" What must he or she think? The same thing occurs when English speakers learn German: They hear a lot of weird expressions that don't seem to make much sense when they look the words up in a dictionary. That's because they're idioms or just plain slang, and direct translations are impossible. Let's take a look at some interesting German phrases and their English idiomatic counterparts:

Das ist mir egal.	I don't care.
Das ist reiner Quatsch!	That's a lot of baloney!
Du nimmst mich auf den Arm.	You're pulling my leg.
Er murmelte etwas in seinen Bart.	He mumbled something under his breath.
Halt's Maul!	Shut up! Hold your tongue!
Hau ab!	Get out! Knock it off!
Ich habe mit ihm ein Hühnchen zu rupfen.	I've got a bone to pick with him.
Mensch! Das ist ja toll!	Man! That's just great!
Mir hängt der ganze Kram zum Halse heraus.	I'm fed up with the whole thing.
Schieß los!	Get going!
Seine Frau ist in andern Umständen.	His wife's in the family way.

CHAPTER 8

Indirect Objects and the Dative Case

Indirect objects are a part of speech you use all the time in English. This chapter will introduce you to the dative case and show you how to make use of it to indicate an indirect object.

What's an Indirect Object?

It may sound like just another confusing grammatical term, but an indirect object is something you are already very familiar with. You use it every day in English. It's really quite simple to identify in a sentence. Ask "for whom" or "to whom" something is being done and the answer is the indirect object. See the following table for some examples in English:

▼ IDENTIFYING INDIRECT OBJECTS

The Sentence	Ask "for whom" or "to whom"	The Indirect Object
He gave her a dollar.	To whom did he give a dollar?	her
We sent them a letter.	To whom did we send a letter?	them
I bought you a ring.	For whom did I buy a ring?	you

Indirect Objects in German

In German the indirect object is indicated by the dative case. Like the accusative case, this case requires changes to the definite and indefinite articles of nouns.

▼ **DEFINITE ARTICLES IN THE DATIVE CASE**

Masculine	Feminine	Neuter	Plural
dem	der	dem	den

Unlike the accusative case, which changed only masculine nouns, all nouns and pronouns make a slight change when used in the dative case. Masculine and neuter words change *der* and *das* to *dem*. Feminine nouns change *die* to *der*. And plural nouns change the article *die* to *den*.

Indefinite articles also take different endings when they are used in the dative case.

▼ **INDEFINITE ARTICLES IN THE DATIVE CASE**

Masculine	Feminine	Neuter	Plural
einem	einer	einem	keinen

In addition to these changes to the definite and indefinite articles, plural nouns also require an ending on the noun itself. In the dative plural, the noun must end with an extra *–n* if there isn't already one in the plural nominative: *mit zwei Heften*. Take a close look at the following examples to see how the dative endings are used in comparison with the nominative and accusative cases.

▼ **THE NOMINATIVE, ACCUSATIVE, AND DATIVE CASES OF NOUNS**

Gender	Nominative	Accusative	Dative
Masculine	der Mann	den Mann	dem Mann
Masculine	ein Mann	einen Mann	einem Mann
Feminine	die Lampe	die Lampe	der Lampe
Feminine	eine Lampe	eine Lampe	einer Lampe
Neuter	das Heft	das Heft	dem Heft
Neuter	ein Heft	ein Heft	einem Heft
Plural	die Hefte	die Hefte	den Heften
Plural	keine Hefte	keine Hefte	keinen Heften

Let's look at some sentences that demonstrate the use of the dative with an indirect object:

Die Männer geben der alten Frau ein Brötchen.
The men give the old lady a bread roll.

Der Vater kaufte seinem Sohn ein Fahrrad.
The father bought his son a bicycle.

Wir kaufen dem Mädchen eine neue Lampe.
We buy the girl a new lamp.

Changing Dative Nouns to Pronouns

You have already learned how to change nominative and accusative nouns to pronouns. The same idea is used when changing dative nouns to pronouns. The key to making the change correctly is identifying the gender of the noun. If the noun is masculine or neuter, change the pronoun to *ihm*. If the noun is feminine, change the pronoun to *ihr*. And if the noun is plural, change the pronoun to *ihnen*. You already know that a noun combined with *ich* (*mein Vater und ich*) is replaced by *wir*. Therefore, if the noun/*ich* phrase is in the dative case, change it to the pronoun *uns*. Let's look at some examples.

▼ **PRONOUNS IN THE DATIVE CASE**

Person	Nominative	Dative	English
First (sing.)	*ich*	*mir*	me
Second (sing.)	*du*	*dir*	you
Third (sing.)	*er*	*ihm*	him
Third (sing.)	*sie*	*ihr*	her
Third (sing.)	*es*	*ihm*	it
First (pl.)	*wir*	*uns*	us
Second (pl.)	*ihr*	*euch*	you all
Second (formal)	*Sie*	*Ihnen*	you
Third (pl.)	*sie*	*ihnen*	them

Notice that the dative forms of *Sie* and *sie* (pl.) are identical except for the capitalization of *Sie* and *Ihnen*.

Some example sentences with dative pronouns as indirect objects:

Er gibt ihr ein Geschenk. (He gives her a gift.) (To whom? Her.)
Wir kaufen ihm einen Hut. (We buy him a hat.) (For whom? Him.)
Ich bringe dir ein Glas Bier. (I bring you a glass of beer.) (To whom?
You.)
Sie geben mir den Teller. (They give me the plate.) (To whom? Me.)

▼ **REPLACING DATIVE NOUNS WITH PRONOUNS**

Noun in the Dative Case	Pronoun Replacement for the Dative Noun
Ich gebe dem Kind einen Bleistift.	*Ich gebe ihm einen Bleistift.* (I give him a pencil.)
Sie tanzt mit meinem Vater.	*Sie tanzt mit ihm.* (She is dancing with him.)
Mark wohnt bei seiner Tante.	*Mark wohnt bei ihr.* (Mark lives with her.)
Er kaufte den Kindern Schokolade.	*Er kaufte ihnen Schokolade.* (He bought them chocolate.)
Sie bekommt einen Brief von Hans und mir.	*Sie bekommt einen Brief von uns.* (She receives a letter from us.)

Sentences Can Be Chock Full of Pronouns!

Have you noticed that sentences that contain an indirect object also have a direct object in them? *Sie gibt ihrem Vater das Buch.* (She gives her father the book.) To whom does she give the book? *Ihrem Vater* is the indirect object. What does she give to her father? *Das Buch* is the direct object.

You've practiced changing either the indirect object noun or the direct object noun to a pronoun. But it's possible to change both to pronouns. You do it in English, but you may add a word when you do so. You place the preposition "to" or "for" in front of the pronoun that has replaced the indirect object. Look at these examples of changing both the direct object and indirect object nouns to pronouns:

Mary sent the man some sandwiches.	Mary sent them **to** him.
We bought Sally a new toy.	We bought it **for** her.
I gave the boys a puppy.	I gave it **to** them.

German doesn't have to add a preposition when changing indirect and direct object nouns to pronouns. But there is a little switch made: The indirect object pronoun changes position with the direct object pronoun. Take a look at some examples:

Ich gebe dem Mann eine Tasse.	*Ich gebe sie ihm.*
Erich kaufte seiner Schwester ein Fahrrad.	*Erich kaufte es ihr.*
Er bringt den Kindern vier Bücher.	*Er bringt sie ihnen.*

Any time the direct object is a pronoun, it will *always* stand before the indirect object.

Karl gibt es seinem Freund.	*Karl gibt es ihm.*
(Karl gives it to his friend.)	(Karl gives it to him.)

Remember the phrase used to ask how someone is? *Wie geht's?* Often people use a pronoun with this expression: "How are _you_?" Of course, you have to know which form of "you" is involved: *du, ihr,* or *Sie.*
Then you can ask:

• *Wie geht es dir?*	How are you? (informal singular)
• *Wie geht es euch?*	How are you? (informal plural)
• *Wie geht es Ihnen?*	How are you? (formal)

Notice that these are dative pronouns. The question *Wie geht es . . . ?* is followed by the dative case, as is the reply: *Es geht mir gut.*

Exercise 8-1
Fill in the blank of each sentence with the dative form of the definite article (*dem, der, den*).

1. *Ich gebe* _____ *Lehrer mein Heft.* (I give the teacher my notebook.)
2. *Er sendet* _____ *Dame einen Brief.* (He sends the lady a letter.)
3. *Frau Schmidt bringt* _____ *Schüler ein Glas Wasser.* (Mrs. Schmidt brings the student a glass of water.)
4. *Wir geben* _____ *Kellner das Geld.* (We are giving the waiter the money.)
5. *Was gibst du* _____ *Studentin?* (What are you giving the student?)

Prepositions That Take the Dative Case

There are also some prepositions in German that change what follows them to the dative case. These are called the dative prepositions.

aus (from, out of)	*nach* (after, to a region)
außer (besides, except)	*seit* (since)
bei (at, by, at the house of)	*von* (from, of)
mit (with)	*zu* (to, towards, to the house of)

The word or phrase that follows one of these prepositions must be in the dative case, which means you would use the dative article (definite or indefinite) or the dative pronoun. These sentences use the dative prepositions.

Ich spreche mit der Frau.	I am speaking with the woman.
Sie wohnen bei Herrn Müller.	They live at the house of Mr. Müller.
Morgen kommt er zu uns.	Tomorrow he is coming to us / to our house.
Wohin gehst du mit dem Hund?	Where are you going with the dog?
Der Arzt fragt nach der kranken Frau.	The doctor asks after the sick woman.
Er hat außer der Schwester auch einen Bruder.	Besides his sister he also has a brother.

The preposition *zu* means "to" or "toward." In German it is often used where in English we say "to someone's house." *Zu mir* means literally "to me" or "toward me." But it can also be translated as "to my house." Other examples are *zu euch* (to you, toward you, to your house) and *zu uns* (to us, toward us, to our house).

Another Use of the Dative Case

In addition to its use with indirect objects and following the dative prepositions you see above, there's another function of the dative case. Certain verbs are called dative verbs. The object that follows them has to be in the dative case. Like a dative preposition, these verbs act as a signal to you to use the dative case. There are several dative verbs, but let's start with these five:

folgen (to follow)	*Der Hund folgt dem Mann nach Hause.*
	(The dog follows the man home.)
gefallen (to please)	*Das gefällt mir nicht.*
	(I don't like that. / That doesn't please me.)
gehören (to belong to)	*Das Haus gehört seinem Bruder.*
	(The house belongs to his brother.)
glauben (to believe)	*Glauben Sie ihr?*
	(Do you believe her?)
helfen (to help)	*Ich helfe einem Freund.*
	(I help a friend.)

German has yet another way of saying that you "like" something, which uses the dative verb *gefallen*. The verb *lieben* expresses that you truly "love" something. *Gern haben* is milder and is comparable to "like." But there's another interesting phrase that is similar to *gern haben*. Its meaning is "to be pleasing": *Es gefällt mir.* (I like it.) Literally, it means "It is pleasing to me."

This is a very commonly used expression. To use it, you have to get used to putting "what you like" at the beginning of the sentence (it is actually the subject of the sentence) and using the dative pronouns after the verb.

▼ USING *GEFALLEN* TO EXPRESS LIKE

English Phrase	German Phrase
Do you like it?	*Gefällt es dir?*
He likes that.	*Das gefällt ihm.*
She likes the books.	*Die Bücher gefallen ihr.*
We like the dress.	*Das Kleid gefällt uns.*
Do you like the play?	*Gefällt euch das Schauspiel?*
Don't you like it?	*Gefällt es Ihnen nicht?*
They don't like the hat.	*Der Hut gefällt ihnen nicht.*

CHAPTER 9

Asking Questions

You've already seen quite a few questions in German in the sections of this book. You know how to ask how someone is doing and what his or her name is. In this chapter you'll have a detailed look at questions and the interrogative words used to ask them.

The Three Types of Questions

German and English share many similarities when it comes to asking questions. There are three ways of doing this:

Intone a statement like a question.
Thomas ist krank? (Thomas is sick?)
Reverse the position of the subject and the verb.
Ist Thomas krank? (Is Thomas sick?)
Begin the sentence with an interrogative word.
Warum ist Thomas krank? (Why is Thomas sick?)

Placing a Verb First

When a sentence is changed to a question, the only change in German is the position of the verb and the subject. It doesn't matter if the subject is a noun or a pronoun. Invert the order of the two so that the verb comes first in the question:

Wir sind hier. (We are here.) / *Sind wir hier?* (Are we here?)
Karl hat ein Buch. (Karl has a book.) / *Hat Karl ein Buch?* (Does Karl have a book?)

It's really quite simple. But because English forms questions in a more complicated way, you might think you have to do something similar in German. In fact, that's not the case. Look at these statements in English:

Thomas has a book. **Does** Thomas have a book?
They go home. **Do** they go home?
She is sick. **Is** she sick?
The boys are in school. **Are** the boys in school?

When you translate English questions into German, they all are formed the same way: The verb comes before the subject. German has no need for "do" or "does" in its formation of questions.

The same thing applies when you negate sentences and questions. Compare the German and English:

▼ QUESTIONS IN THE NEGATIVE

English Question	German Question
Isn't he sick?	*Ist er nicht krank?*
Aren't you in school?	*Bist du nicht in der Schule?*
Don't I know him?	*Kenne ich ihn nicht?*
Doesn't she have a book?	*Hat sie kein Buch?*

 Alert

Remember, to negate an indefinite article like *ein*, you must use the *kein* form of the article, not *nicht*. *Kein* negates a noun, which is why it changes according to the gender, case, and number of the noun. *Kein* always comes before the noun.

With nearly all English verbs, questions are formed by beginning the question with "do" or "does." This never happens in German. "To be" is one of the few English verbs that doesn't require "do" or "does" to form a question: Is she at home? Are you alone?

Interrogative Words

Another way to form a question is to use an interrogative (or question) word. There are several interrogative words, and each one asks something different. Notice that even when a question begins with an interrogative word (who? what? how?), the verb still comes before the subject in the sentence.

Ist Hans da?	Is Hans there?
Sind Sie Amerikanerin?	Are you an American?
Heißen Sie Schmidt oder Braun?	Is your name Schmidt or Braun?
Wie heißen Sie?	What is your name? (Literally: How are you called?)
Wo ist Herr Weber?	Where is Mr. Weber?
Wer ist das?	Who is that?

▼ INTERROGATIVE WORDS

The Kind of Question	The Interrogative	The Question	A Possible Answer
where someone is	*wo?*	*Wo ist dein Vater?* (Where is your father?)	*Er ist zu Hause.* (He is at home.)
where someone is going	*wohin?*	*Wohin geht Hans?* (Where is Hans going?)	*Er geht ins Kino.* (He is going to the movies.)
where someone is coming from	*woher?*	*Woher kommst du?* (Where do you come from?)	*Ich komme aus Amerika.* (I come from America.)
who someone is	*wer?*	*Wer ist er?* (Who is he?)	*Er ist der Lehrer.* (He is the teacher.)
how someone does something	*wie?*	*Wie spielt er Tennis?* (How does he play tennis?)	*Er spielt gut Tennis.* (He plays tennis well.)

The Kind of Question	The Interrogative	The Question	A Possible Answer
when something is done	*wann?*	*Wann kommst du nach Hause?* (When are you coming home?)	*Ich komme um elf Uhr nach Hause.* (I'm coming home at eleven o'clock.)
what something is	*was?*	*Was hast du?* (What do you have?)	*Ich habe einen neuen Hut.* (I have a new hat.)
what kind of	*was für?*	*Was für ein Buch ist das?* (What kind of book is that?)	*Das ist ein Lehrbuch.* (That is a textbook.)
why something is done	*warum?*	*Warum ist er müde?* (Why is he tired?)	*Er ist sehr alt.* (He is very old.)

Asking Where

The German language has three specific forms of the question "where?": *wo, wohin,* and *woher.*

The three forms are really three different concepts about location. *Wo* always asks at what location a person is. *Wohin* asks to what location a person is going. And *woher* wants to know from what location someone or something comes.

Wo asks "where" someone or something is: *Wo bist du jetzt?* (Where are you now?) By using the preposition *in,* you can give a large variety of answers to the question "where?" when you use city and country names. Many are the same in both English and German: *in Berlin, in Bonn, in New York, in Amerika, in Deutschland.*

Wo ist Liese? (Where is Liese?) *Sie ist in London.* (She is in London.)
Wo bist du? (Where are you?) *Du bist in Berlin.* (You are in Berlin.)

The question word *wohin* is used to ask where someone is going with verbs of motion:

Wohin gehst du? (Where are you going?) Wohin fliegen Sie? (Where are you flying?) Wohin fährst du? (Where are you driving?)

If the destination is the thing you want to question, you have to ask not just "where?" but "where to?" Use *wohin* in this case.

Wohin fährt der Kellner? (Where's the waiter driving?)
Der Kellner fährt nach Schweden. (The waiter is driving to Sweden.)

What if you're asking where someone or something comes from? That's when you need the third question word for "where?" *Woher* asks "from where?" *Woher kommst du?* (Where do you come from?)

 **Question**

Are there different kinds of verbs to be used with the three meanings of "where?"
Any verb that shows location at a place can be used with *wo* (*Wo wohnt er?* [Where does he live?]). But with *wohin* and *woher*, use verbs of motion: *Wohin gehen/fahren/fliegen Sie?* (Where are you going/driving/flying?) *Woher kommt er?* (Where is he coming from?)

Asking How and When

Adverbs—whether in German or English—tell you something about the verb: how, where, or when something is done. Use *wie* to ask "how" and *wann* to ask "when."

You have already used several adverbial phrases: *Es geht Andreas gut.* (Andreas is doing well.) *Heute gehe ich nach Hause.* (Today I am going home.) *Im Winter ist es kalt.* (In winter it is cold.) Here are a few more practical adverbs to add to your vocabulary:

- *langsam* (slowly)
- *leise* (quietly)
- *laut* (loudly)
- *schnell* (fast)

Let's look at some sample questions and answers using *wie* and *wann*.

Wie fährt dein Bruder? (How does your brother drive?)
Er fährt sehr schnell. (He drives very fast.)

Wann kommt Tina? (When is Tina coming?)
Sie kommt heute. (She's coming today.)

Wann ist das Konzert? (When is the concert?)
Das Konzert ist morgen. (The concert is tomorrow.)

Asking Who

To ask who someone is, use the interrogative *wer* (who). *Wer ist das?* means "Who is that?"

Wer ist der Mann? Der Mann ist Herr Schmidt.
Who is the man? The man is Mr. Smith.

Wer ist das Mädchen? Das Mädchen ist Petra.
Who is the little girl? The little girl is Petra.

Wer ist die Frau? Die Frau ist Professorin Klein.
Who is the woman? The woman is Professor Klein.

Wer sind die Kinder? Die Kinder sind Karl und Monika.
Who are the children? The children are Karl and Monika.)

Alert

Be careful of forming questions from sentences with two subjects. The question words take singular verbs. If two people are the subject, the question you ask is still *wer*. But, just like the English word "who," the German word *wer* is singular. The same thing is true of *was* (what). Examples: (a) *Wer ist da?* (Who is there?) *Peter und Karl sind da.* (Peter and Karl are there.) (b) *Was ist da?* (What is there?) *Das Hotel und die Post sind da.* (The hotel and the post office are there.)

Wer is slightly different from the other question words in that it can change form to show case, like the personal pronouns.

Asking What Kind or Why

Was für asks about the characteristics of someone or something: color, size, quality. *Was für ein Mädchen ist sie?* (What kind of a girl is she?) *Sie ist ein sehr intelligentes Mädchen.* (She's a very smart girl.) Don't confuse *was für* with *was*, which asks only "what."

The word for why is *warum*. This question asks for a reason. The English response to why (*warum?*) something is done is given with the conjunction "because": "Why did he leave her?" "He left her <u>because</u> they fell out of love." One German word for "because" is *denn*. *Warum geht er nach Hause?* (Why is he going home?) *Er geht nach Hause, <u>denn</u> er ist müde.* (He is going home because he's tired.) Use *denn* to show the reason for some action.

 Fact

Punctuation rules vary a bit from English to German. You often do not need to use a comma before the word "because" in English, but in German you always use a comma before *denn*.

Exercise 9-1

Ask questions based on the sentences given below. Use the <u>underlined</u> phrase in each sentence to decide what kind of question to form.

1. *Ich kaufe <u>einen neuen Volkswagen</u>.* (I buy a new Volkswagen.)

2. *Morgen gehen wir in <u>die Bibliothek</u>.* (Tomorrow we are going to the library.)

3. *Der Student sucht <u>ein Heft und zwei Bleistifte</u>.* (The student is looking for a notebook and two pens.)

4. *Am Donnerstag fliegen sie nach New York.* (On Thursday we're flying to New York.)

---

5. *Sabine findet eine graue Bluse.* (Sabine finds a gray blouse.)

The Other Cases of *wer*

Unlike the other interrogatives, *wer* is a pronoun that changes according to case. When asking "who" or "whom," you have to know what case is involved: nominative, accusative, or dative. And if you wish to question ownership (the possessive adjective), you have to use "whose."

Wer wohnt da?	Who lives there?
Wen besuchen Sie?	Whom are you visiting?
Mit wem fahren Sie?	Who are you going with?
Wessen Haus ist das?	Whose house is that?

Let's look at the possibilities.

▼ ASKING QUESTIONS WITH WHO, WHOM, AND WHOSE

English Meaning	German Interrogative	Usage in a Sentence	Example
who?	*wer?*	subject	*Wer wohnt in Bayern?* (Who lives in Bavaria?)
whom?	*wen?*	accusative direct object	*Wen besuchen Sie in der Stadt?* (Whom are you visiting in the city?)
whom?	*wen?*	after an accusative preposition	*Für wen ist das Geschenk?* (Who is the gift for?)
whom?	*wem?*	dative indirect object	*Wem gibst du das Glas?* (Who do you give the glass to?)
whom?	*wem?*	after a dative preposition	*Von wem sprecht ihr?* (About whom are you all speaking?)

English Meaning	German Interrogative	Usage in a Sentence	Example
whose?	*wessen?*	replacing a possessive adjective	*Wessen Schwester liebt er?* (Whose sister does he love?)
whose?	*wessen?*	replacing a possessive adjective	*Wessen Buch nimmt er?* (Whose book is he taking?)

It is common for English speakers to use "who" where "whom" is needed. Don't let that tendency cause you to use the wrong form of *wer*. Always decide how "who" is being used, then use the appropriate German form.

Using *wen*

Wen means "whom" and is used to ask about nouns referring to people when they are used as direct objects. It's just like English.

▼ USING *WEN* TO ASK "WHOM"

Underlined Direct Object	Question with *wen*
Sie sehen den Mann. (You see the man.)	*Wen sehen Sie?* (Whom do you see?)
Sie sehen die Lehrerin. (You see the teacher.)	*Wen sehen Sie?* (Whom do you see?)
Ich kenne den Schüler. (I know the pupil.)	*Wen kenne ich?* (Whom do I know?)
Ich kenne das Mädchen. (I know the girl.)	*Wen kenne ich?* (Whom do I know?)

The Dative Case with the Forms of *wer*

The signals to use the dative case act on the interrogative *wer* just like the accusative signals.

▼ USING *WER* IN THE DATIVE CASE

Pronoun	Function	Question
wem	dative indirect object	*Wem gibst du das Geld?* (Whom are you giving the money to?)

Pronoun	Function	Question
wem	dative verb	*Wem helfen sie?* (Whom are they helping?)
wem	dative verb	*Wem folgt er nach Hause?* (Whom does he follow home?)
wem	dative verb	*Wem glaubst du nicht?* (Whom don't you believe?)
wem	dative verb	*Wem gehören die Bücher?* (Whom do the books belong to?)
wem	dative verb	*Wem gefällt das neue Hemd?* (Who likes the new shirt?)

When you ask a question about a pronoun that follows a dative preposition, you have to use the preposition with the interrogative word *wem* (whom): *bei wem, mit wem, nach wem, von wem, zu wem.*

▼ USING *WEM* TO ASK "WHOM"

Dative Preposition Underlined	Question
Hans spricht mit ihr. Hans speaks with her.	*Mit wem spricht Hans?* With whom is Hans speaking?
Das ist ein Geschenk von ihnen. That is a gift from them.	*Von wem ist das Geschenk?* From whom is the gift?
Gerda wohnt bei uns. Gerda lives with us.	*Bei wem wohnt Gerda?* With whom does Gerda live?
Sie fragt nach euch. She asks about you all.	*Nach wem fragt sie?* Whom is she asking about?

Exercise 9-2

Form a question based on the phrase underlined in each sentence. For example, when presented with the phrase *Ich spreche mit Karl,* you say *Mit wem spreche ich?*

1. *Er glaubt dir nicht.*

   _____

2. *Sabine kommt mit Tina und Peter.*

   _____

3. *Die Kinder folgen der Mutter.*

_____

4. *Herr Braun wohnt bei meiner Schwester.*

_____

5. *Der Professor fragt nach uns.*

_____

6. *Martin tanzt [dances] mit Andrea.*

_____

7. *Das ist ein Brief [letter] von meinem Vater.*

_____

8. *Stefan hilft mir nicht.*

_____

9. *Das Buch gefällt uns nicht.*

_____

10. *Peter gibt dem Mann das Geld.*

_____

CHAPTER 10

The Numbers Game

Now that you've gotten the basics of sentence formation down, it's time to take a look at numbers in German. Numbers are crucial—you use them every day, not only for counting, but also in addresses, dates, distances, and measurements such as weight. Let's get started.

Starting at Zero

Knowing how to use numbers in German is important. You may already have heard people counting in German, and now it's your turn to take a crack at German numbers. The first thing you'll want to learn is to count to ten.

▼ NUMDCNO 0 10

Arabic Numeral	German Number	Pronunciation
0	*null*	(NOOL)
1	*eins*	(AYNTZ)
2	*zwei*	(TSVY)
3	*drei*	(DRY)
4	*vier*	(FEAR)
5	*fünf*	(**FUE**NF)
6	*sechs*	(ZEX)
7	*sieben*	(ZEE-ben)
8	*acht*	(AH**CH**T)
9	*neun*	(NOIN)
10	*zehn*	(TSAYN)

You have already encountered *ein* and *eine*, which are the German indefinite articles. It is obvious that they come from the German word for "one." You use *eins* as "one" only when counting or when the number stands alone. Once it stands in front of a noun, the –s is dropped and it is treated just like *ein* and *eine*, the indefinite articles. Therefore, *ein Mann* can mean either "a man" or "one man."

Look at some sentences that use the numbers one through ten.

Hier wohnen zwei Amerikaner.
Two Americans live here.

Der alte Mann hat zehn Wagen.
The old man has ten cars.

Sechs Schüler fahren mit dem Bus zur Schule.
Six pupils take the bus to school.

The Next Ten

The next ten numbers are just as simple to use as the first ten. You'll see that the numbers thirteen through nineteen use a combination of *zehn* (ten) and one of the numbers you just learned.

▼ NUMBERS 11–20

Arabic Numeral	German Number	Pronunciation
11	*elf*	(ELF)
12	*zwölf*	(TSV**ERL**F)
13	*dreizehn*	(DRY-tsayn)
14	*vierzehn*	(FEAR-tsayn)
15	*fünfzehn*	(**FUE**NF-tsayn)
16	*sechzehn*	(ZEX-tsayn)
17	*siebzehn*	(ZEEP-tsayn)
18	*achtzehn*	(AH**CH**T-tsayn)
19	*neunzehn*	(NOIN-tsayn)
20	*zwanzig*	(TSVAHN-tsik)

Note that in *sechzehn* the number *sechs* has dropped the letter –*s*, and in *siebzehn* the number *sieben* has dropped the syllable –*en*.

Let's look at some simple equations in German. For addition, you can use either the word *plus* (which means the same thing in German as it does in English) or *und* (which means "and"). For subtraction, German uses the words *minus* (just like English, again!) or *weniger* (which means "less" or "minus"). When asking the question "how much," you say *wie viel* (vee-FEEL).

$6 + 3 = 9$	*Sechs plus drei ist neun.*
$9 + 4 = 13$	*Neun und vier ist dreizehn.*
$17 - 5 = 12$	*Siebzehn minus fünf ist zwölf.*
$9 - 2 = 7$	*Neun weniger zwei ist sieben.*
Wie viel ist zwei plus zwei?	How much is two plus two?
Wie viel ist sechs und zwei?	How much is six and two?
Wie viel ist neun weniger drei?	How much is nine minus three?

Multiplication and division are simple also. In order to multiply two numbers, you use *mal* (times). Look at a few examples.

Drei mal drei ist neun.	Three times three is nine.
Vier mal zwei ist acht.	Four times two is eight.
Zwei mal zwei ist vier.	Two times two is four.
Fünf mal zwei ist zehn.	Five times two is ten.

For division of numbers, say the phrase *geteilt durch* (geh-TYLT DOORCH).

Vier geteilt durch zwei ist zwei.	Four divided by two is two.
Neun geteilt durch drei ist drei.	Nine divided by three is three.
Zehn geteilt durch zwei ist fünf.	Ten divided by two is five.
Acht geteilt durch vier ist zwei.	Eight divided by four is two.

The Rest of the Numbers

The numbers from one to twenty are the basis for learning the rest of the numbers in German. To make that process easier, keep in mind a line from a children's rhyme: "Four and twenty blackbirds baked in a pie." As you learn the numbers above twenty, you'll see why this rhyme is fitting for putting together numbers in German. First let's look at the numbers for counting by tens to 100.

 Fact

In German numbers, commas and periods are reversed compared to the American style of writing numbers. For instance, 100.000 in German means 100,000. Likewise, a comma is used to separate cents from Euros in currency, for example *5,50 EUR*.

▼ **COUNTING BY TENS**

Arabic Numeral	German Number	Pronunciation
10	*zehn*	(TSAYN)
20	*zwanzig*	(TSVAHN-tsik)
30	*dreißig*	(DRY-sik)
40	*vierzig*	(FEAR-tsik)
50	*fünfzig*	(**FUE**NF-tsik)
60	*sechzig*	(ZEK-tsik)
70	*siebzig*	(ZEEP-tsik)
80	*achtzig*	(AH**CH**-tsik)
90	*neunzig*	(NOIN-tsik)
100	*hundert*	(HOON-duhrt)

Just as happened in the teens, *sechzig* has dropped the letter *–s* from *sechs*, and in *siebzig* the syllable *–en* has been omitted from *sieben*.

The hundreds are even easier to form. Note that with the hundreds, the forms of *sechs* and *sieben* do not drop any letters.

▼ **THE HUNDREDS**

Arabic Numeral	German Number
100	*hundert*
200	*zweihundert*
300	*dreihundert*
400	*vierhundert*
500	*fünfhundert*
600	*sechshundert*
700	*siebenhundert*
800	*achthundert*
900	*neunhundert*
1,000	*tausend*

This pattern follows in the thousands: *zweitausend, zehntausend*, etc.

Here's where the blackbirds come in: With twenty-one through ninety-nine, the numbers one through nine are placed before the rest of the number and connected by *und*.

einundzwanzig	21, literally "one-and-twenty"
zweiundzwanzig	22
dreiundzwanzig	23
vierunddreißig	34
fünfundfünfzig	55
sechsundsiebzig	76
siebenundneunzig	97

When using *eins*, don't forget to drop the *–s* in this formation of numbers: *einundvierzig, einundachtzig*.

 Alert

Here's some interesting news. No matter how long the number gets, German numbers are written as one word: 701 is written *siebenhunderteins*, the year 1776 is *siebzehnhundertsechsundsiebzig*; 3582 is *dreitausendfünfhundertzweiundachtzig*. For that reason, Germans tend to avoid writing out numbers and prefer to write the numerals.

The larger numbers in German—*Million, Milliard, Billion*—are almost identical to English. (But be on guard: There's one notable exception.) These larger numbers are capitalized. The other numbers are not.

▼ NUMBERS FOR BILLIONAIRES

English Number	German Number	Example
million	*eine Million* (mee-lee-OHN)	*zehn Millionen Dollar*
billion	*eine Milliarde* (mee-lee-AHR-deh)	*drei Milliarden EUR*
trillion	*eine Billion* (bee-lee-OHN)	*sechs Billionen Pesos*

Careful! If you're a billionaire, you have to be aware of how German and English differ when it comes to billions and trillions. Take another look at the table and check out the meaning of *Milliarde* and *Billion*.

Street Addresses and Phone Numbers

There are actually two ways to say the number "two" in German. You already know *zwei*. But there is another form of that number, and it is a very close relative to the English number two. The other German form is *zwo* (TSVOH). The two forms can be used interchangeably, but *zwo* is usually used to be clear about the number that is meant. It is often used to give a precise figure. Telephone numbers sometimes are spoken with *zwo*.

For example, if your telephone number in Germany is 82 21 45, you would tell someone your number by saying, "*Meine Telefonnummer ist acht zwei, zwei eins, vier fünf.*" (My telephone number is eight two, two one, four five.) To be a bit more precise, you could say, "*Meine Telefonnummer ist acht zwo, zwo eins, vier fünf.*" Notice that the numbers are generally said in pairs.

 **Essential**

In Germany, it is common to answer the telephone by saying your last name as an introduction. For example, you could answer the phone with *Schmidt* or *Schmidt am Apparat* (Schmidt on the phone). You will often hear *das Handy* used when referring to a cell phone. The proper name is *das Mobiltelefon*.

If you wish to give your area code, you say, "*Die Vorwahl ist null, vier, zwei.*" (The area code is zero, four, two.) Or you could say, "*Die Vorwahl ist null, vier, zwo.*"

The same use of *zwei* or *zwo* is possible when giving an address. It all has to do with wishing to give precise numbers to someone (i.e., avoiding confusion because *zwei* and *drei* rhyme). In German addresses, the number is usually said after the street: *Hauptstraße 9.*

But, like English, German uses more than the word *Straße* (street) in addresses. They sometimes also use *Allee* (lane) or *Chaussee* (from the French word for road). And there are numerous specialized phrases used for street names. Look at the examples in the following table:

▼ GERMAN STREET ADDRESSES

Address	Pronunciation of the Number
Buchwaldstraße 9	*neun* (NOIN)
Schlüterstraße 24	*vierundzwanzig* (fear-oont-TSVAHN-tsik)
Rothenbaumchaussee 32	*zweiunddreißig* (tsvy-oont-DRY-sik)
Bahnhofallee 5	*fünf* (**FUE**NF)
Kurfürstendamm 12	*zwölf* (TSV**ER**LF)
Neue Kantstraße 2	*zwei* (TSVY) or *zwo* (TSVOH)
Westring 10	*zehn* (TSAYN)
Kaiserdamm 11	*elf* (ELF)

When giving an address, normally the zip code and city come first, followed by the street address. When addressing an envelope, use the same format but place the name of the recipient above the zip code and city. Look at some examples of complete addresses together with telephone numbers for northeastern Germany (*Vorwahl* [area code]: 0049).

 Alert

When dialing a phone number within Germany, you need to dial a 0 before the city code. For example, a telephone number would look like 040-433 99 66. It's similar to the U.S. practice of dialing a 1 before the area code.

▼ **ADDRESSES WITH CITY, STREET, AND TELEPHONE NUMBER**

Zip Code	City	Street Address	Telephone Number
12106	Berlin	Schlossstraße 72	0049 – 40 – 433 99 66
20240	Hamburg	Maienweg 509	0049 – 30 – 322 31 12
22082	Hamburg	Langenhorner Chaussee 56	0049 – 30 – 221 88 54
24331	Kiel	Sophienblatt 133	0049 – 431 – 591 44
21862	Stade	Pferdemarkt 119	0049 – 4141 – 13 20

There is a slight difference between the English version of an address and a German version. The sender's address is placed in the upper left hand corner just like in English. The first line is often the abbreviation *Abs.*, which stands for *Absender* (the sender of the letter). This is followed by the name of the sender, the sender's street address, and the sender's *Postleitzahl* (zip code), city, and country (if in a different country). The sender's address would look like this:

Felix Schneider
Bahnhofstr. 25
20466 Hamburg
(Deutschland)

 Fact

In most cases in the German-speaking world, the street number follows the street name (*Kaiserallee 11*). And when writing from one German-speaking country to another, the letters *D*, *A*, and *Ch* precede the *Postleitzahl* to identify Germany, Austria, and Switzerland respectively (*A-4922 Waldzell*).

The addressee's address on an envelope is similar in form and appears in the center of the envelope just as in English. But the addressee should be addressed by his or her title (*Herr, Frau, Professor*, etc.) on the first line. The addressee's name appears on the second line and then street address, *Postleitzahl* and city, with the optional country last.

For example:

Herrn
Friedrich Schiller
Kaiserallee 11
A-4922 Waldzell
Österreich

Expressing Quantities

Have you noticed that In German the word "of" doesn't occur in certain expressions that require it in English? Where we say "a cup of coffee," German does without the preposition "of": *eine Tasse Kaffee*. There are many examples of this kind of expression.

ein Glas Bier	a glass of beer
zwei Glas Bier	two glasses of beer
ein Liter Milch	a liter of milk
drei Liter Milch	three liters of milk
ein Meter Wolle	one meter of wool
vier Meter Seide	four meters of silk
eine Tasse Tee	a cup of tea
acht Tassen Tee	eight cups of tea
eine Kanne Wasser	a pitcher of water
zwei Kannen Wasser	two pitchers of water
eine Flasche Wein	a bottle of wine
sechs Flaschen Wein	six bottles of wine

Did you notice that the feminine nouns above changed to the plural with the numbers *acht* and *zwei*? You say *eine Tasse Kaffee* and *eine Kanne Wasser*, but with numbers larger than one, you use the plural: *acht Tassen Kaffee* and *zwei Kannen Wasser*. Masculine and neuter nouns do not change to the plural in this instance: *ein Glas Bier, zwei Glas Bier*.

Measuring the Metric Way

The German-speaking countries, like all of Europe, use the metric system exclusively. When you go into a store in Germany, you can't ask for a quart of milk or two yards of yellow ribbon. You need to know *Liter* and *Meter.*

The metric system is really quite efficient, because it's based on numbers that are easily multiplied and divided (1, 10, 100, 1,000):

- *ein Kilometer* (1 kilometer) equals *eintausend Meter* (1,000 meters)
- *ein Meter* (1 meter) equals *einhundert Zentimeter* (100 centimeters)
- *ein Meter* (1 meter) equals *eintausend Millimeter* (1,000 millimeters)

Using metrics you can measure distance, length, weight, temperature, and volume.

Distance and Length

In the United States, we judge long distances in miles. The metric equivalent is *Kilometer,* which equals a thousand meters. Shorter distances are measured by yards, feet, and inches in English. In the metric system, shorter lengths are measured by *Meter, Zentimeter,* and *Millimeter. Ein Kilometer* is about 0.6 miles. To know how far *sechs Kilometer* is, multiply six times 0.6. That's 3.6 miles. These metric lengths are usually abbreviated to *km, m, cm,* and *mm.*

Weight

Americans measure weight by pounds and ounces. Americans have sixteen ounces in one pound. In the metric system, weight measurements are calculated in easy multiples: *ein Kilogramm* (1 kilogram) equals *eintausend Gramm* (1,000 grams).

The German word *Pfund* means pound, but it's not the pound we know in the United States. *Ein Pfund* is *fünfhundert Gramm* (500 grams) or half a *Kilogramm. Kilogramm* is abbreviated as *kg, Gramm* as *g.* German speakers often just say *Kilo* instead of *Kilogramm: Ich möchte ein Kilo Tomaten, bitte.* (I'd like a kilogram of tomatoes, please.) *Ein Kilo* is about 2.2 pounds. So if you want to know how many pounds *drei Kilo* are, multiply three times 2.2. That's 6.6 pounds.

Temperature

Americans use the Fahrenheit thermometer to measure temperature: 212°F is the boiling point of water, and 32°F is its freezing point. The metric system (Celsius) once again works in simpler multiples. *Einhundert Grad* (100 degrees) is the boiling point of water, and *null Grad* (0 degrees) is the freezing point.

 Fact

To convert temperatures from Celsius to Fahrenheit, multiply the metric temperature by 9, divide by 5, and add 32. To find the temperature in Fahrenheit of *zweiundzwanzig Grad* Celsius (22°C), multiply 22 by 9/5. Then add 32. That tells you that it's 71.6°F.

Volume

In the United States, liquids are measured in pints, quarts, and gallons. In the metric system, liquids are measured by *Liter* and *Milliliter*. If you want to know how many fluid ounces *vierzig Milliliter* (40 milliliters) are, multiply forty times 0.034. That comes to 1.36 fluid ounces. To know how many quarts are in *zehn Liter* (10 liters), multiply ten times 1.06. That's 10.6 quarts. To find pints, multiply the number of liters by 2.1. To find gallons, multiply the number of liters by 0.26.

Ordinal Numbers

There's another aspect to German numbers. The numbers you've learned so far are the cardinal numbers: *eins, zwei, drei, zwanzig, vierhundert, achttausend, eine Million*. There are also ordinal numbers, which act as adjectives.

In English, ordinal numbers are formed by adding –*th* to a cardinal number: fifth, sixth, twentieth, hundredth, and so on. In this respect, German is very similar to English. Some ordinals are formed by adding –*te* to the cardinal number. With numbers twenty and greater, ordinals have an –*ste* ending.

zweite	(second)	*achte*	(eighth)
vierte	(fourth)	*neunte*	(ninth)
fünfte	(fifth)	*zehnte*	(tenth)
sechste	(sixth)	*elfte*	(eleventh)
siebte	(seventh)	*neunzehnte*	(nineteenth)
zwanzigste	(twentieth)	*achtzigste*	(eightieth)
dreißigste	(thirtieth)	*neunzigste*	(ninetieth)
vierzigste	(fortieth)	*hundertste*	(hundredth)
fünfzigste	(fiftieth)	*dreihundertste*	(three-hundredth)
sechzigste	(sixtieth)	*tausendste*	(thousandth)
siebzigste	(seventieth)		

And just like English, German has exceptions to these rules:

erste   (first)   *dritte*   (third)   *siebte*   (seventh)

Remember that ordinals are adjectives. The *–e* ending shown in the previous example is only one adjective ending. The ordinal numbers take different adjective endings depending on number, gender, and case. Let's look at some other possibilities:

▼ ORDINALS AND ADJECTIVE ENDINGS

German Phrase	English Meaning
die ersten drei Jahre	the first three years
mein zweiter Sohn	my second son
am siebzehnten April	on the seventeenth of April
das einundzwanzigste Kapitel	the twenty-first chapter
der dritte Mai	the third of May

How about Fractions?

German fractions are nouns. They have to be capitalized just like other nouns. For numbers up to nineteen, just add –*tel* to the cardinal number. For numbers twenty and above, the ending becomes –*stel*.

▼ **FRACTIONS**

Arabic	German	English
⅓	*ein Drittel*	one-third
¼	*ein Viertel*	one-fourth
⅕	*ein Fünftel*	one-fifth
⅙	*ein Sechstel*	one-sixth
⅒	*ein Zehntel*	one-tenth
¹⁄₁₃	*ein Dreizehntel*	one-thirteenth
¹⁄₁₉	*ein Neunzehntel*	one-nineteenth
¹⁄₂₀	*ein Zwanzigstel*	one-twentieth
¹⁄₃₀	*ein Dreißigstel*	one-thirtieth
¹⁄₈₀	*ein Achtzigstel*	one-eightieth
¹⁄₁₀₀	*ein Hundertstel*	one-hundredth

The only word that doesn't follow this pattern of nouns ending in –*tel* or –*stel* is the word "half." In German, *halb* is an adjective and takes the regular adjective endings: *Ich möchte ein halbes Brot.* (I'd like half a loaf of bread.) *Geben Sie mir bitte einen halben Kuchen!* (Give me half a cake, please.)

There is also a noun for half, but it's not used in fractions: *die Hälfte.* Use it in expressions like *um eine Hälfte teurer* (half again as expensive) and *bessere Hälfte* (better half, i.e., a spouse).

There are some special compounds of fractions that are always said in their own special way.

▼ *HALB* **AND COMPOUND FRACTIONS**

Arabic Fraction	German	English
1½	*anderthalb*	one and a half
2½	*zweieinhalb*	two and a half
3½	*dreieinhalb*	three and a half
¾	*dreiviertel*	three-fourths

Compound Numerals

These expressions are identical in German and English and are used in the same way in both languages. *Mal* means "times" and *Fach* means "fold." Look how they combine with numbers to form compounds.

▼ COMPOUND NUMERALS

German	English	German	English
einmal	once, one time	hundertmal	hundred times
zweimal	twice, two times	einfach	single, simple
dreimal	thrice, three times	zweifach	double, twofold
viermal	four times	dreifach	threefold
fünfmal	five times	zehnfach	tenfold
zehnmal	ten times	hundertfach	hundredfold
dreißigmal	thirty times		

Accurate use of numbers and numerals will make your German sound more authentic. And practice makes perfect! *Übung macht den Meister!*

Meet the Euro

Most of continental Europe is using the Euro as its official currency. That includes Germany and Austria, but not Switzerland. There are 100 *Cent* in one *Euro*, which corresponds easily to 100 cents in a dollar, and which makes understanding European money quite simple. Compare the following:

▼ DOLLARS AND EUROS

American Dollars and Cents	European Euro and Cent
$5.50	5,50 €
$10.95	€ 10,95
$1.25	1,25 €

Be aware that you will see the sign for Euro (€) placed either in front of or in back of the amount of money. Sometimes the letters *EUR* or the symbol € are used with money amounts. You'll encounter both: *€ 3,15* and *3,15 EUR.*

Prices are said with the Euro amount first and followed by the number of *Cent.* For *6,10 €* and *2,05 €* you would say *Sechs Euro und zehn Cent* and *Zwei Euro und fünf Cent.* You can ask how much something costs by asking, *Wie viel kostet das?* (How much does that cost?) The reply might be something like: *Das kostet zwei Euro und fünf Cent.*

Exercise 10-1

Ask how much each object costs. Use the price to give the answer. For example, when presented with the words *der Mantel 10,00 EUR*, you ask *Wie viel kostet der Mantel?* Then reply, *Der Mantel kostet zehn Euro.*

1. *das Brötchen*   *2,10 EUR*

   _____

   _____

2. *die Lampe*   *7,10 EUR*

   _____

   _____

3. *der Teller und die Tasse*   *10,00 EUR*

   _____

   _____

4. *das Gemüse*   *4,10 EUR*

   _____

   _____

5. *die Milch*   *3,05 EUR*

   _____

   _____

CHAPTER 11

Telling Time

Knowing how to talk about time—hours, days, weeks, months, and so on—is essential to using the German language. In the following sections you'll learn how to talk about time.

Time of Day

You've already used the adverb *morgen* (tomorrow) with some verbs to indicate something that is going to happen in the future. The term *der Morgen* is very similar but is a noun that means "morning." Here are some important words to know to talk about the time of day:

der Abend (evening)	*die Nacht* (night)
der Morgen (morning)	*der Tag* (day)
der Vormittag (morning)	*der Nachmittag* (afternoon)

When you talk about the times of day, you use certain words to tell whether they are in the past, present, or future. For example, in English we say "yesterday morning," "this morning," "tomorrow morning." Those expressions are also used for most of the other times of day. Take a careful look at what happens in German and compare it to English.

▼ **THE TIMES OF DAY IN GERMAN**

German Expression	English Expression
gestern Abend	yesterday evening
gestern Morgen	yesterday morning
gestern Nachmittag	yesterday afternoon
gestern Nacht	last night
heute Abend	this evening
heute Morgen	this morning
heute Nachmittag	this afternoon
heute Nacht	tonight
morgen Abend	tomorrow evening
morgen früh	tomorrow morning
morgen Nachmittag	tomorrow afternoon
morgen Nacht	tomorrow night
übermorgen	the day after tomorrow
vorgestern	the day before yesterday

Don't confuse *Morgen*, the noun that means "morning," with *morgen*, the adverb that means "tomorrow."

Exercise 11-1

Using the two phrases provided, ask when someone is coming. Answer with the provided adverb. For example:

Peter / morgen
Wann kommt Peter? Er kommt morgen.

1. *Tante Luise / übermorgen* _____
2. *der Professor / heute Nachtmittag* _____
3. *Frau Keller / heute Abend* _____
4. *Martin / morgen früh* _____
5. *Herr Schäfer / heute Morgen* _____
6. *Kinder / morgen Abend* _____

Hours and Minutes

What if you need to be more specific than "yesterday evening" or "this afternoon?" You'll need to use the clock to indicate a specific time. The word *die Uhr* means "the clock." But the same word is placed after time to mean "o'clock." There are a few kinds of clocks and watches in German, and they typically end with *–uhr* (note the exception in this list):

die Armbanduhr	wristwatch
die Taschenuhr	pocket watch
die Wanduhr	wall clock
der Wecker	alarm clock

When time is on the hour, you merely say the number and follow it by *Uhr*: *ein Uhr* (1:00 A.M.), *zwei Uhr* (2:00 A.M.), *drei Uhr* (3:00 A.M.), *sieben Uhr* (7:00 A.M.), *zwölf Uhr* (12:00 A.M.), *dreizehn Uhr* (1:00 P.M.), *achtzehn Uhr* (6:00 P.M.), *zwanzig Uhr* (8:00 P.M.), *einundzwanzig Uhr* (9:00 P.M.), *zweiundzwanzig Uhr* (10:00 P.M.), *dreiundzwanzig Uhr* (11:00 P.M.), *vierundzwanzig Uhr* (twelve midnight).

 Fact

Did you know that Germans usually use the military clock when they tell time? They don't use A.M. or P.M. They show 3:00 P.M. as *15.00 Uhr*. They also use a period where we would use a colon in writing the time.

The times that occur between the top of the hour and the half hour all come *nach* (after).

1:10	*zehn nach eins* (ten past one)
4:20	*zwanzig nach vier* (twenty past four)
6:15	*Viertel nach sechs* (a quarter past six)

If the time is thirty minutes after the hour, use the word *halb* (half) and the next hour. Think of it as being "halfway" to the next hour.

| 2:30 | *halb drei* (two-thirty) |
| 9:30 | *halb zehn* (nine-thirty) |

If the times occur between the half hour and the three-quarter hour, use *nach* followed by the expression for the half hour.

| 3:35 | *fünf Minuten nach halb vier* (five minutes past three-thirty, or 3:35) |
| 7:40 | *zehn Minuten nach halb acht* (ten minutes past seven-thirty, or 7:40) |

Germans often leave out the word *Minuten*: *zehn nach halb acht* (ten past seven-thirty). It's also correct to simply state the hour and minutes. For example, *sieben Uhr vierzig* is an acceptable way to say it's 7:40. Telling time in German differs from region to region and there are lots of variations, but using the hour and minute is one universally valid and easily understood way.

From a quarter before the hour to the top of the next hour, use *vor* (before).

| 12:45 | *Viertel vor eins* (a quarter to one) |
| 4:50 | *zehn Minuten vor fünf / zehn vor fünf* (ten before five) |

Asking for the Time

To ask what time it is, use one of these expressions: *Wie viel Uhr ist es?* (What time is it?) or *Wie spät ist es?* (How late is it?) Some possible responses are:

Es ist halb zehn.	It's 9:30 (A.M).
Es ist neunzehn Uhr.	It's 7:00 P.M.
Es ist Viertel vor sieben.	It's a quarter to seven.
Es ist zwei Uhr.	It's two o'clock.

To ask at what time something occurs, precede the time by the preposition *um*. Note the use of *um* in these questions and answers.

▼ USING *UM* WHEN TELLING TIME

Question	Answer
Um wie viel Uhr kommt der Zug? (At what time does the train come?)	*Der Zug kommt um vierzehn Uhr.* (The train comes at 2:00 P.M.)
Um wie viel Uhr ist die Prüfung? (At what time is the exam?)	*Die Prüfung ist um halb neun.* (The exam is at 8:30 [A.M.].)
Um wie viel Uhr gehen Sie nach Hause? (At what time are you going home?)	*Ich gehe um elf Uhr nach Hause.* (I am going home at eleven o'clock.)

Just like English, German has special words for "noon" and "midnight": *Mittag* (literally "midday") and *Mitternacht*. They are used in place of twelve o'clock:

Es ist jetzt zwölf Uhr.	It is now twelve o'clock.
Es ist jetzt Mittag.	It is now noon.
Er kommt um Mitternacht.	He comes at midnight.

Exercise 11-2
Using the two phrases provided, ask what time an event is. Answer with the time provided. For example:

die Party / 2.00
Um wie viel Uhr ist die Party? Die Party ist um zwei Uhr.

1. *der Film / 15.00* _____
2. *die Prüfung / 10.30* _____
3. *das Fußballspiel* (soccer match) */ 16.45* _____
4. *das Konzert* (concert) */ 20.15* _____
5. *die Geburtstagsparty* (birthday party) */ 13.00* _____

Days of the Week

The days of the week are all masculine nouns because they are compound words formed with the word *der Tag* (except for the word for Wednesday).

▼ DAYS OF THE WEEK

German	English	German	English
Sonntag	Sunday	Donnerstag	Thursday
Montag	Monday	Freitag	Friday
Dienstag	Tuesday	Sonnabend/Samstag	Saturday
Mittwoch	Wednesday		

Take note of how the days of the week are used in the following questions and answers.

> Ist heute Montag? Ja, heute ist Montag.
> Ist heute Samstag? Nein, heute ist Freitag.
> Ist heute Montag oder Dienstag? Heute ist Montag.
> Ist heute Mittwoch oder Donnerstag? Heute ist Donnerstag.

The days of the week are used in an adverbial phrase when preceded by the preposition *am* (contraction of *an dem*). Then they tell "when" something occurs.

> Wann ist das Konzert (concert)? Das Konzert ist am Montag.
> Wann ist die Party? Die Party ist am Sonnabend.
> Wann kommt Herr Meyer? Herr Meyer kommt am Freitag.
> Wann gehst du nach Hause? Ich gehe am Donnerstag nach Hause.

When an adverb that tells "when" is in the middle of a sentence, it stands before a phrase that tells "where."

Wir fahren _heute_ in die Stadt.	We are driving to the city today.
Hans fliegt _morgen_ in die Alpen.	Hans is flying to the Alps tomorrow.
Ich bin _am Dienstag_ in der Schule.	I am in school on Tuesday.

Exercise 11-3

Using the two phrases provided, ask when an event is. Answer with the day provided. For example:

die Party / Montag   *Wann ist die Party? Die Party ist am Montag.*

1. *das Konzert / Sonntag* _____
2. *der Film / Dienstag* _____
3. *die Oper* (opera) / *Mittwoch* _____
4. *das Schauspiel* (play) / *Donnerstag* _____
5. *das Examen / Freitag* _____

The Seasons of the Year

Some of the German words for the seasons of the year are similar to the English words.

▼ SEASONS OF THE YEAR

German	English	German	English
der Sommer	summer	*der Winter*	winter
der Herbst	fall	*der Frühling*	spring

And, like English, they are used very frequently with the preposition *in*. But in German, you have to say "in the" season and use the contraction *im: im Sommer, im Herbst, im Winter, im Frühling.*

If you begin a sentence with one of the seasons, remember to place the verb before the subject: *Im Winter sind wir in Florida.*

Herzlichen Glückwunsch zum Geburtstag!

It's a mouthful, but that's how you say "happy birthday" in German. Naturally, it will be helpful to know the German months if you're going to talk about birthdays.

German months are very similar to their English counterparts, but remember that in German they are all masculine.

▼ MONTHS OF THE YEAR

German	English	German	English
Januar	January	Juli	July
Februar	February	August	August
März	March	September	September
April	April	Oktober	October
Mai	May	November	November
Juni	June	Dezember	December

They are used in exactly the same way as the English months: in January (*im Januar*), in May (*im Mai*), in September (*im September*). Notice, however, that German uses *im* (the contraction of *in dem*) in place of *in*.

To tell what month you were born in, just say: *Ich bin im Februar geboren.* (I was born in February.) *Ich bin im Juni geboren.* (I was born in June.) You can change the verb *sein* appropriately to say what month others were born in: *Vater ist im Oktober geboren.* (Father was born in October.) *Die Zwillinge sind im März geboren.* (The twins were born in March.) *Wann bist du geboren?* (When were you born?)

And if you want to say that something occurred in a certain year, you say *im Jahre: im Jahre 1776, im Jahre 2009. Ich bin im Jahre 1985 geboren.* (I was born in 1985.)

And if you want to tell in what month your birthday is, you say, *Ich habe im April Geburtstag.* (I have a birthday in April.) *Er hat im Juli Geburtstag.* (He has a birthday in July.)

The word *Geburtstag* (birthday) is used in a variety of ways. Look at all the things you can say:

▼ A BIRTHDAY PARTY

German Expression	English
Geburtstagskind	birthday girl or boy
Geburtstagsparty	birthday party
Geburtstagskuchen	birthday cake
den Geburtstagskuchen probieren	to try or taste the birthday cake
die Kerzen ausblasen	to blow out the candles
den Geburtstag feiern	to celebrate the birthday

Exercise 11-4

Using the name and the year provided, form a sentence that says when someone was born. For example, when presented with *Peter/1990*, you say *Peter ist im Jahre 1990 geboren*.

1. *Frau Keller / 1961* _____
2. *das Baby / 2008* _____
3. *meine Schwester / 1989* _____
4. *meine Großmutter / 1939* _____
5. *Herr Schmidt / 1978* _____

Adjectives and the Accusative Case

When you place an adjective before a day, the word *die Woche* (week), a month, or the word *das Jahr* (year), the phrase has to be in the accusative case. That's important for masculine nouns, because remember that the article changes from *der* to *den*. Note that the gender and accusative case are indicated by endings on the adjectives here.

▼ TIME EXPRESSIONS WITH ADJECTIVES

German Expression	English Expression
letzten Montag	last Monday
letzten Dienstag	last Tuesday
letzten Mittwoch	last Wednesday
diesen Donnerstag	this Thursday
diesen Freitag	this Friday
diesen Sonnabend	this Saturday
nächsten Sonntag	next Sunday
nächsten Montag	next Monday
nächsten Freitag	next Friday
letzte Woche	last week
diese Woche	this week
nächste Woche	next week
letzten Januar	last January
diesen Mai	this May

German Expression	English Expression
nächsten August	next August
letztes Jahr	last year
dieses Jahr	this year
nächstes Jahr	next year

Using Ordinals to Give Dates

Both English and German express dates by using ordinal numbers: the first of May, the tenth of September, from June fourth until July eleventh, and so on.

When you want to know the date in German, you ask, *Der Wievielte ist heute?* The response is, *Heute ist der erste April. Heute ist der achte August. Heute ist der einundzwanzigste November.* Each time the adjective ending is *−e*, because with *Der−* words in the nominative, the adjective ending is always an *−e*.

But if you ask the exact date on which something occurred, you use *am* (*an dem*) before the ordinal, which requires an *−en* adjective ending: *am zehnten März, am zweiundzwanzigsten Januar, am dreißigsten Juli.*

▼ EXPRESSING DATES

German Question	German Answer	English
Der Wievielte ist heute?	Heute ist der zehnte Juni.	Today is the tenth of June.
Der Wievielte war gestern?	Gestern war der dritte Februar.	Yesterday was the third of February.
Wann ist er geboren?	Er ist am zwanzigsten April geboren.	He was born on the twentieth of April.

CHAPTER 12

Talking about the Past

By now you know how to conjugate quite a few verbs and how to talk about time in days, months, seasons, and years. So far this book has concentrated on things happening in the present time. In the following sections you'll learn how to use verbs to talk about things that happened in the past.

The Regular Past Tense

You can undoubtedly tell from the title that German must have an "irregular" past tense somewhere. Don't let it worry you. Fortunately for you as an English speaker, you have the advantage of knowing very similar past tense patterns in your native language.

For now you're just going to concentrate on the regular past tense. In English, the regular past tense is when you tack on the ending –*ed* to a verb and it takes on a past tense meaning.

he jumps	he jumped
we look	we looked
I travel	I traveled

Just think of all the English verbs that form their past tense by this simple method. The German method is just as easy. Just add –*te* to the stem of the verb and it becomes past tense.

▼ FORMING THE PAST TENSE

Infinitive	Verb Stem	Past Tense
spielen (to play)	*spiel*	*spielte*
fragen (to ask)	*frag*	*fragte*
suchen (to search)	*such*	*suchte*

If the stem of the verb ends in *−t* or *−d*, you have to add an extra *−e* before placing the past tense ending *−te* on the end of the stem:

warten (to wait)   *wart*   *wartete*

After you have formed the past tense (*spielte, fragte, suchte, wartete*), you're not quite done. As with all German verbs, the conjugational ending must still be added. But notice that the endings for *ich, er, sie*, and *es* are the same: *−te*. The past tense conjugation of regular verbs will look like the ones in the following table.

▼ CONJUGATING THE PAST TENSE

Pronoun	spielen	fragen	warten
ich	*spielte*	*fragte*	*wartete*
du	*spieltest*	*fragtest*	*wartetest*
er, sie, es	*spielte*	*fragte*	*wartete*
wir	*spielten*	*fragten*	*warteten*
ihr	*spieltet*	*fragtet*	*wartetet*
Sie	*spielten*	*fragten*	*warteten*
sie (pl.)	*spielten*	*fragten*	*warteten*

There are no new conjugational endings to learn for the past tense. This past tense formation is called *das Imperfekt* in German. It is used primarily to show that something was done often (*Sie spielte oft Tennis.* / She played tennis often.) or in a narrative that describes events that happen in sequence. Remember that English has two present tense forms: I drive / I am driving. Both English forms become just one form in German: *ich fahre.* The same is true in the past tense. English has two forms; German has one.

English Past Tenses	German Past Tense
we were learning	*wir lernten*
we learned	*wir lernten*

Exercise 12-1

Form the past tense for the following regular verbs with the pronouns provided. For example:

spielen   ich __*spielte*__   du __*spieltest*__   wir __*spielten*__

1. *sagen* (say)   *ich* _____   *sie* (s.) _____   *sie* (pl.) _____
2. *kaufen* (buy) *du* _____   *es* _____   *wir* _____
3. *stellen* (put)   *ich* _____   *ihr* _____   *Sie* _____
4. *reisen* (travel) *du* _____   *er* _____   *wir* _____
5. *baden* (bathe)   *er* _____   *ihr* _____   *Sie* _____

Forming Questions in the Past Tense

It is easy to ask questions in the past tense. There is no special formula for forming past tense questions. What you already know about questions in the present tense also applies to the past tense.

In most German questions the verb comes before the subject: *Hast du einen Hund?* (Do you have a dog?) This is true even when an interrogative word begins the sentence: *Was hast du?* (What do you have?) For past tense questions, merely use the proper form of the verb conjugated in the past tense.

▼ CONTRASTING PRESENT TENSE AND PAST TENSE QUESTIONS

Present Tense	Past Tense
Spielst du Tennis?	*Spieltest du Tennis?*
(Do you play tennis?)	(Did you play tennis?)
Brauchen Sie Geld?	*Brauchten Sie Geld?*
(Do you need money?)	(Did you need money?)
Hören Sie Radio?	*Hörten Sie Radio?*
(Do you listen to the radio?)	(Did you listen to the radio?)

Present Tense	Past Tense
Lernst du Deutsch?	*Lerntest du Deutsch?*
(Are you learning German?)	(Did you learn German?)
Wo wohnt er?	*Wo wohnte er?*
(Where does he live?)	(Where did he live?)
Wer arbeitet hier?	*Wer arbeitete hier?*
(Who works here?)	(Who worked here?)
Wen besucht er?	*Wen besuchte er?*
(Whom is he visiting?)	(Whom did he visit?)
Was kauft ihr?	*Was kauftet ihr?*
(What are you all buying?)	(What did you all buy?)

The Past Tense of Irregular Verbs

There is a long list of German verbs that form the past tense by irregular stem formations. That sounds like trouble, but for English speakers it's really not so bad. These verbs are often called "strong verbs." In this book they're just going to be called "irregular."

What you already know about the past tense will help you to use irregular verbs in the past. Regular verbs simply put a *–te* on the end of the stem of the verb. Then the conjugational ending is added. But irregular verbs do something different, and it's exactly what irregular verbs do in English: They form a completely new stem. Let's look at some examples in English.

▼ **VERB STEMS OF THE ENGLISH IRREGULAR PAST TENSE**

Infinitive	Past Tense Stem	Infinitive	Past Tense Stem
to come	came	to bring	brought
to see	saw	to drive	drove
to run	ran	to go	went

Once you know the past tense stem, you can use it with any number of subjects.

Pronoun	Present Tense	Past Tense	Pronoun	Present Tense	Past Tense
I	sing	sang	we	sing	sang
you	sing	sang	they	sing	sang
he, she, it	sings	sang			

Take note that the third person singular (he, she, it) requires an –s ending in the English present tense. There are no endings in the past tense.

If you think about it, you can come up with a very long list of irregular verbs in English. If you are a native speaker of English, you know them because you slowly absorbed them during your childhood. You use them automatically without thinking that you have to make some kind of strange stem change in order to give a particular verb a past tense meaning. Native speakers of English have a treasury of irregular verb stems tucked away in their brains.

Comparing English and German in the Past Tense

As English-speaking kids grow up, they make mistakes. Little Johnny might say, "I drinked all my milk, Mom." But he's only five years old. In time, he'll know that the past tense of "drink" is "drank."

Kids who grow up speaking German do the same thing. For a while they form all their past tense verbs like regular verbs, with a –te ending. But eventually they begin to remember the irregularities and use the past tense of these verbs correctly.

And you will do the same thing. You'll discover that German irregular past tense forms follow the pattern of English past tense forms very closely.

Let's look at a list of some frequently used verbs so you can see what happens in both languages.

▼ IRREGULAR VERBS IN ENGLISH AND GERMAN

English Infinitive	Past Tense Stem	German Infinitive	Past Tense Stem
to break	broke	brechen	brach
to bring	brought	bringen	brachte
to come	came	kommen	kam
to drink	drank	trinken	trank

English Infinitive	Past Tense Stem	German Infinitive	Past Tense Stem
to fly	flew	*fliegen*	*flog*
to go	went	*gehen*	*ging*
to see	saw	*sehen*	*sah*
to sing	sang	*singen*	*sang*
to speak	spoke	*sprechen*	*sprach*
to stand	stood	*stehen*	*stand*

Remember that the simple past tense (*das Imperfekt*) is used in narratives and to show repetition.

What are some of the verbs that require stem changes in the past tense? The following table is a list of some common verbs that are irregular in the past tense. Notice how many of them follow a pattern similar to the English past tense.

▼ **IRREGULAR PAST TENSE STEMS**

English Infinitive	German Infinitive	Past Tense Stem
to bake	*backen*	*buk (or backte)*
to be called	*heißen*	*hieß*
to become	*werden*	*wurde*
to catch	*fangen*	*fing*
to drive	*fahren*	*fuhr*
to eat	*essen*	*aß*
to fall	*fallen*	*fiel*
to find	*finden*	*fand*
to give	*geben*	*gab*
to have	*haben*	*hatte*
to help	*helfen*	*half*
to hit	*schlagen*	*schlug*
to know	*wissen*	*wusste*
to know, be acquainted	*kennen*	*kannte*
to let	*lassen*	*ließ*
to meet	*treffen*	*traf*
to read	*lesen*	*las*
to run	*laufen*	*lief*

English Infinitive	German Infinitive	Past Tense Stem
to sleep	*schlafen*	*schlief*
to take	*nehmen*	*nahm*
to think	*denken*	*dachte*
to wash	*waschen*	*wusch*
to wear, carry	*tragen*	*trug*
to write	*schreiben*	*schrieb*

Conjugations in the German Irregular Past Tense

You recall from previous chapters that German verbs always have to have conjugational endings. That's also true in the irregular past tense. You already know those endings.

▼ **IRREGULAR PAST TENSE CONJUGATIONS**

Pronoun	kommen	gehen	sehen
ich	*kam*	*ging*	*sah*
du	*kamst*	*gingst*	*sahst*
er/sie/es	*kam*	*ging*	*sah*
wir	*kamen*	*gingen*	*sahen*
ihr	*kamt*	*gingt*	*saht*
Sie	*kamen*	*gingen*	*sahen*
sie (pl.)	*kamen*	*gingen*	*sahen*

As you can see, there's nothing new about the conjugation of the irregular past tense. Once you know the stem, you merely use the endings you already know.

Did you notice that, like in the past tense of regular verbs, the pronouns *ich, er, sie,* and *es* do not add a conjugational ending to the stem?

Exercise 12-2

Fill in the correct past tense form of the verb in parentheses.

1. *Meine Tante (wohnen)* _____ *in den Vereinigten Staaten.*
   (My aunt lived in the United States.)

2. *Ich (lieben)* _____ *Brot mit Käse.* (I loved bread and cheese.)

3. *Wohin (fliegen)* _____ *ihr?* (Where did you all fly to?)

4. *Ihr (spielen)* _____ *oft Fußball.* (You all played soccer often.)

5. *Ich (hören)* _____ *keine Musik.* (I didn't listen to any music.)

6. *Sie* (sing.) *(gehen)* _____ *ins Kino.* (She went to the movies.)

7. *(sprechen)* _____ *du mit Thomas?* (Did you speak with Thomas?)

8. *Er (sehen)* _____ *Frau Schmidt im Büro.* (He saw Ms. Schmidt in the office.)

9. *Die Kinder (antworten)* _____ *auf Französisch.* (The children answered in French.)

10. *Wir (singen)* _____ *auf Deutsch.* (We sang in German.)

The Importance of Being

The infinitive *sein* is a very important verb. It's used as frequently in German as "to be" is used in English. You are very familiar with it in the present tense. But now it's time to become familiar with its past tense.

Just like the English "to be," the German *sein* makes a complete transformation in the past tense. "To be" becomes "was." *Sein* becomes *war.* You'll find that, like other irregular verbs, conjugating *war* is a snap.

▼ THE PAST TENSE OF *SEIN*

Person	English	German
First (sing.)	I was	*ich war*
Second (sing.)	you were	*du warst*
Third (sing.)	he/she/it was	*er/sie/es war*
First (pl.)	we were	*wir waren*
Second (pl.)	you all were	*ihr wart*
Second (formal)	you were	*Sie waren*
Third (pl.)	they were	*sie waren*

A Special Look at *haben* and *werden*

These are two very frequently used verbs in German. When used on their own, they mean "to have" and "to become," respectively. But they have another use: These verbs, along with *sein*, will be used to form the perfect. Watch out for these two! *Haben* and *werden* are irregular in both the present and past tenses.

▼ THE PAST TENSE OF *HABEN*

Person	Conjugation	Person	Conjugation
First (sing.)	*ich hatte*	First (pl.)	*wir hatten*
Second (sing.)	*du hattest*	Second (pl.)	*ihr hattet*
Third (sing.)	*er/sie/es hatte*	Second (formal)	*Sie hatten*
		Third (pl.)	*sie hatten*

▼ THE PAST TENSE OF *WERDEN*

Person	Conjugation	Person	Conjugation
First (sing.)	*ich wurde*	First (pl.)	*wir wurden*
Second (sing.)	*du wurdest*	Second (pl.)	*ihr wurdet*
Third (sing.)	*er/sie/es wurde*	Second (formal)	*Sie wurden*
		Third (pl.)	*sie wurden*

CHAPTER 13

Look to the Future

Knowing the past tense is great for talking about things that have already happened. But what about the plans you're making for next summer or even next weekend? In this chapter you'll learn how to use the future tense. You'll also learn how to use the imperative form of verbs to give commands. Ready? Go!

What Are You Doing Tomorrow?

The future tense is simple to use. In many cases, you just use a present tense conjugation in a context that implies a future tense meaning.

Heute geht Karl in die Schule.	Karl's going to school today.
Morgen geht Karl in die Schule.	Karl's going to school tomorrow.

But just as English has a more specific way of forming the future tense, so does German. Its formation is very much like English. In English you simply use the verb "shall" or "will" and follow it with the verb that describes what will be done in the future:

I go there.	I shall go there.
You are late.	You will be late.
Mother has a problem.	Mother will have a problem.

Fact

Nowadays, particularly in spoken English, people usually use "will" in the future tense. Although "shall" is a proper form and has a specific usage, you'll find only "will" used here with the English future tense.

Using *werden*

The other way to form the future tense is really quite simple. It has to do with another use of a verb you already know: *werden*. To form the future tense, conjugate *werden* and follow it with the infinitive that describes what will be done in the future. But be careful! In German the infinitive has to be the last word in the sentence—no matter how long the sentence might be. How about some examples?

Er wird nach Hause gehen.
He will go home.

Die Kinder werden morgen im Park spielen.
Tomorrow the children will play in the park.

Ich werde am Sonnabend in die Stadt fahren.
I will drive to the city on Saturday.

Exercise 13-1

Change the present tense sentences below to the future tense by using *werden*. For example, when presented with the sentence *Ich bleibe in Berlin* (I am staying in Berlin), you say, *Ich werde in Berlin bleiben.* (I will stay in Berlin.)

1. *Die Männer spielen Fußball.* (The men are playing soccer.)

   _____

2. *Er wohnt in Bayern.* (He lives in Bavaria.)

   _____

3. *Meine Freunde sind in den Alpen.* (My friends are in the Alps.)

---

4. *Ich denke oft an Heinrich.* (I often think of Heinrich.)

---

5. *Was brauchen Sie?* (What do you need?)

---

6. *Sabine arbeitet im Kaufhaus.* (Sabine works in the department store.)

---

7. *Ich kaufe nur Milch.* (I only buy milk.)

---

8. *Was machst du?* (What are you doing?)

---

9. *Er sagt etwas.* (He says something.)

---

10. *Wir sprechen nur Deutsch.* (We speak only German.)

Present, Past, and Future

You have already become acquainted with three important tenses in German. Now you can speak about anything that has happened, is happening, or will happen.

Three of the most important "signal" words that tell you what tense to use are *heute* (today), *gestern* (yesterday), and *morgen* (tomorrow). *Heute* is the signal for the present tense, *gestern* for the past tense, and *morgen* for the future tense. Let's look at how the three tenses differ in form and meaning with regular verbs.

 Alert

Did you remember that English has two tense forms for each tense? For each of those pairs, German always has only one tense.

Tense	English	German
Present	I am learning German.	*Ich lerne Deutsch.*
Present	I learn German.	*Ich lerne Deutsch.*
Past	I was learning German.	*Ich lernte Deutsch.*
Past	I learned German.	*Ich lernte Deutsch.*
Future	I will be learning German.	*Ich werde Deutsch lernen.*
Future	I will learn German.	*Ich werde Deutsch lernen.*

Look at the sentences below and notice how the three tenses differ in verb formation and usage.

Present: *Heute bin ich in der Hauptstadt.*
(I am in the capital city today.)

Past: *Gestern war ich in der Hauptstadt.*
(I was in the capital city yesterday.)

Future: *Morgen werde ich in der Hauptstadt sein.*
(I will be in the capital city tomorrow.)

Future Tense with Irregular Verbs

Because in the future tense you use *werden* plus an infinitive, the irregular verbs are very easy to use in the future tense. There's no stem change to remember. When you form the future tense of any verb, you conjugate *werden* and place the accompanying verb as an infinitive at the end of the sentence. That means you have to change any irregularity in the present tense back to the verb's infinitive form when restating a sentence in the future tense.

▼ CONTRASTING THE PRESENT AND FUTURE TENSES OF IRREGULAR VERBS

Present Tense	Future Tense
Er liest die Zeitung.	*Er wird die Zeitung lesen.*
He reads the newspaper.	He will read the newspaper.

Present Tense	Future Tense
Sie läuft in die Schule.	*Sie wird in die Schule laufen.*
She runs to school.	She will run to school.
Sabine trägt einen neuen Hut.	*Sabine wird einen neuen Hut tragen.*
Sabine is wearing a new hat.	Sabine will wear a new hat.
Das Kind spricht kein Deutsch.	*Das Kind wird kein Deutsch sprechen.*
The child doesn't speak any German.	The child will not speak any German.
Andreas fängt den Ball.	*Andreas wird den Ball fangen.*
Andreas catches the ball.	Andreas will catch the ball.
Wo trifft sie die Touristen?	*Wo wird sie die Touristen treffen?*
Where is she meeting the tourists?	Where will she meet the tourists?

Exercise 13-2

Restate each future tense sentence in the present tense. For example:

Sie wird es verstehen. _____ Sie versteht es. _____

1. *Die Kinder werden Deutsch lernen.*

   _____

2. *Ich werde mit ihm sprechen.*

   _____

3. *Helga wird oft an uns denken.*

   _____

4. *Wirst du in Bremen wohnen?*

   _____

5. *Erik wird nach Hause laufen.*

   _____

Giving Orders

The imperative is quite simple in German. But first, let's look at how an order or a command is given in English. You can take any infinitive (to run, to hide, to spell), drop the word "to," and you have an imperative form:

Run to the store.
Hide in the bushes.
Spell the word correctly.

German is a bit different, but equally easy. We'll start with the formal command form. Begin with an infinitive: *gehen*. Place the pronoun *Sie* (formal you) behind it, and you have the German imperative: *Gehen Sie!* (Go!) Note that the German imperative always requires an exclamation point after it. Only one verb requires a little spelling change to form the imperative: *sein*. An *–e* is added after the letter *i*. Then follow the word with *Sie* and you have: *Seien Sie!* (Be!). Here are a few examples:

Bleiben Sie da! (Stay there.)   *Fahren Sie schneller!* (Drive faster.)
Essen Sie! (Eat.)   *Fliegen Sie nach Berlin!* (Fly to Berlin.)

Informal Commands

In addition to the *Sie* (formal) version of commands, there are ways to give commands to those whom you know on a less formal basis, using the two other words for "you" in German: *du* and its plural, *ihr*. You cannot use the formal command with people to whom you say *du*. There are informal imperative formations, and they are really quite simple. For informal singular (*du*), take the stem of the verb and add *–e*:

Gehe! (Go.) *Bleibe!* (Stay.) *Komme!* (Come.)

 Fact

It is very common to drop the final *–e* in a *du*-imperative. Instead of saying *Gehe!* you can say *Geh!* A few more examples: *Laufe! = Lauf! Komme! = Komm! Bestelle! = Bestell!*

If the verb is irregular and has a vowel change in the present tense (*–e* to *–i* or *–ie*), make that change in the verb stem, but do not add an *–e* on the end:

Gib! (Give.) *Sprich!* (Speak.) *Sieh!* (See.) *Sei!* (Be.)

For the informal plural (*ihr*), just use the regular present tense conjugation without the pronoun. It's also the imperative of the verb:

Geht! (Go.)   *Sprecht!* (Speak.)   *Bleibt!* (Stay.)
Seid! (Be.)   *Seht!* (See.)

Let's compare how the three different forms of the imperative form work.

▼ COMPARING THE FORMS OF THE IMPERATIVE

Infinitive	Command for *du*	Command for *ihr*	Command for *Sie*	English
suchen	Suche!	Sucht!	Suchen Sie!	Seek. / Look for.
fahren	Fahre!	Fahrt!	Fahren Sie!	Drive.
singen	Singe!	Singt!	Singen Sie!	Sing.
essen	Iss!	Esst!	Essen Sie!	Eat.
lesen	Lies!	Lest!	Lesen Sie!	Read.
helfen	Hilf!	Helft!	Helfen Sie!	Help.

Naturally, commands are given politely in German just as they are in English. The word *bitte* (please) is commonly used with the imperative:

Bleibe stehen, bitte!   Remain standing, please.
Iss langsam, bitte!   Eat slowly, please.
Sprecht bitte lauter!   Speak louder, please.
Fahren Sie bitte schnell!   Drive fast, please.

Exercise 13-3
Change the following infinitives to the three types of imperative.

Infinitive	*du*-form	*ihr*-form	*Sie*-form
1. *machen*	_____	_____	_____
2. *trinken*	_____	_____	_____

3. *lesen*   _____   _____   _____
4. *ansehen*   _____   _____   _____
5. *versprechen*   _____   _____   _____
6. *warten*   _____   _____   _____
7. *besuchen*   _____   _____   _____
8. *mitkommen*   _____   _____   _____
9. *schreiben*   _____   _____   _____
10. *glauben*   _____   _____   _____

CHAPTER 14

Perfect Tenses

You know how to form the simple past and the future tenses now. But there's another way to talk about the past and the future. This chapter will introduce you to some very useful tenses that you know well in English—the present perfect, past perfect, and future perfect. Don't let those technical terms scare you! German and English are so similar that the concepts will be a breeze to pick up.

The Present Perfect Tense with *haben*

The present perfect tense in German is formed just like the present perfect tense in English. In English, the present perfect consists of the verb "have" with a past participle. What's a past participle? With regular English verbs it looks just like the past tense:

hurry/hurried   look/looked   play/played

But irregular verbs take on a new form to create a participle:

buy/bought   go/gone   see/seen   speak/spoken

When you combine the verb "have" with a past participle, you have the English present perfect tense. Look at the examples in the following table.

▼ FORMATION OF THE PRESENT PERFECT TENSE IN ENGLISH

Infinitive	Past Tense	Present Perfect Tense
to go	they went	they have gone
to help	he helped	he has helped
to run	she ran	she has run
to play	I played	I have played

German does the very same thing. You conjugate *haben* and follow it with a past participle. But how do you form a German past participle? It's quite easy. If you're working with a regular verb, drop the *–en* from the infinitive to get the stem: *kaufen* becomes *kauf*. Then add the prefix *ge–* and the suffix *–t* to the stem: *kauf* becomes *gekauft*. Now you have a past participle.

Conjugated form of *haben* + past participle = present perfect tense

Be careful: If the stem of the verb ends in *–t* or *–d*, you have to add an extra *–e* before affixing the suffix. For example, the past participle of *antworten* is *geantwortet*.

Let's look at some other examples of regular verbs as past participles.

▼ FORMATION OF REGULAR GERMAN PAST PARTICIPLES

Infinitive	Stem	Prefix *ge–* and Suffix *–t*	Infinitive	Stem	Prefix *ge–* and Suffix *–t*
arbeiten (to work)	*arbeit*	*gearbeitet*	*sagen* (to say)	*sag*	*gesagt*
fragen (to ask)	*frag*	*gefragt*	*spielen* (to play)	*spiel*	*gespielt*
hören (to hear)	*hör*	*gehört*	*suchen* (to search)	*such*	*gesucht*
leben (to live)	*leb*	*gelebt*	*warten* (to wait)	*wart*	*gewartet*
lernen (to learn)	*lern*	*gelernt*	*wohnen* (to live)	*wohn*	*gewohnt*
machen (to do)	*mach*	*gemacht*			

Exercise 14-1

Change the following infinitives to past participles.

1. *kaufen* (to buy) _____
2. *stören* (to disturb) _____
3. *lehren* (to teach) _____
4. *bauen* (to build) _____
5. *stellen* (to place) _____
6. *setzen* (to set) _____
7. *reden* (to talk) _____
8. *baden* (to bathe) _____
9. *lachen* (to laugh) _____
10. *weinen* (to cry) _____

When you use a form of the verb *haben* with the past participle, you have formed the present perfect tense.

ich habe gewohnt	I have lived
er hat gesagt	he has said
du hast gespielt	you have played

There is a slight difference between German and English when it comes to this tense. When Germans want to express something in the past, they tend to use the present perfect tense: *Er hat ein Haus gekauft.* In English, however, people tend to use the simple past tense: He bought a house.

Do you recall how the future tense is formed by conjugating *werden* and placing an infinitive at the end of the sentence? The present perfect tense works the same way—the past participle goes at the end of the sentence.

Future: *Andreas wird morgen Fußball spielen.*
(Andreas will play soccer tomorrow.)

Present Perfect: *Andreas hat gestern Fußball gespielt.*
(Andreas played soccer yesterday.)

Here are a few examples in German of sentences that use the present perfect tense.

Wir haben Deutsch und Spanisch gelernt.	We learned German and Spanish.
Wo haben Sie gewartet?	Where did you wait?
Hast du Schach gespielt?	Did you play chess?
Ich habe eine Stimme gehört.	I heard a voice.
Wem haben Sie den Brief geschickt?	To whom did you send the letter?
Was habt ihr gesagt?	What did you all say?

Oh, Those Darned Irregularities!

Yes, German has irregular past participles just like English. But you'll find that the German irregular past participles tend to be the same ones that we have in English. They are not all the same, but many are.

The formation of the past participle requires knowing the stem changes of irregular verbs. To the irregular stem you add the prefix *ge–* and the suffix *–en*. Look at the steps in forming these past participles.

sprechen/sproch/gesprochen (spoken)
lesen/les/gelesen (read)
singen/sung/gesungen (sung)
helfen/holf/geholfen (helped)
brechen/broch/gebrochen (broken)

Once you have the irregular past participle, you use it the same way you did the regular past participles: Conjugate *haben* and place the past participle at the end of the sentence.

▼ **FORMATION OF IRREGULAR GERMAN PAST PARTICIPLES**

Infinitive	Stem	Prefix *ge–* and Suffix *–en*	English
backen	*back*	*haben gebacken*	have baked
essen	*gess*	*haben gegessen*	have eaten
fangen	*fang*	*haben gefangen*	have caught

Infinitive	Stem	Prefix *ge–* and Suffix *–en*	English
finden	*fund*	*haben gefunden*	have found
geben	*geb*	*haben gegeben*	have given
lassen	*lass*	*haben gelassen*	have let
nehmen	*nomm*	*haben genommen*	have taken
schlafen	*schlaf*	*haben geschlafen*	have slept
schlagen	*schlag*	*haben geschlagen*	have hit
schreiben	*schrieb*	*haben geschrieben*	have written
sehen	*seh*	*haben gesehen*	have seen
tragen	*trag*	*haben getragen*	have worn, carried
treffen	*troff*	*haben getroffen*	have met
trinken	*trunk*	*haben getrunken*	have drunk
waschen	*wasch*	*haben gewaschen*	have washed
bringen	*brach*	*haben gebracht*	have brought
denken	*dach*	*haben gedacht*	have thought
kennen	*kann*	*haben gekannt*	have known, acquainted
wissen	*wuss*	*haben gewusst*	have known

 Alert

Did you notice that the last four verbs in the previous table couldn't make up their minds if they're regular or irregular? They make a stem change but add a *–t* suffix instead of an *–en* suffix. And, yes, the participle for *essen* is *gegessen* with an extra *g* placed before the stem— one more German peculiarity!

Verbs That Use *sein* with Participles

Many people have trouble following the dialogue in a Shakespearean play. The major reason for that is not the general vocabulary of the language used in Shakespeare's time, but the verbs.

English has changed a lot since Shakespeare's lifetime. Among other things, English speakers no longer use "thou," "thy," "thine," or the conjugations that go with "thou." Nowadays many theatergoers have to listen carefully to understand a line such as, "Couldst thou but linger a moment longer." It's not a question, and it simply means, "I wish you'd stay a couple of minutes more." And there is the famous, "Wherefore art thou Romeo?" That is a question, but Juliet doesn't want to know where Romeo is. She's looking right into his face when she says it. She wants to know why he has to be called Romeo—a member of the family considered to be enemies by her kin! How about this one? "His Majesty just this moment is come from the hunt." Does the combination of the words "is come" strike you as strange?

Speakers of modern English usually get the gist of such lines, but sometimes it takes some extra thought. The reason is simple: Modern English conjugations are simpler, and there are no longer two auxiliary verbs in the present perfect tense.

 Essential

In earlier times, certain verbs used "have" with a past participle to form the present perfect tense—just like today. But other verbs—verbs of motion—used "to be" with a past participle to form the present perfect, for example, from the King James version of the Bible, "He is risen." That sentence in modern English would be "He has risen."

The point is that German isn't doing something wacky in the present perfect tense when it uses the verb *sein* with a past participle. It's just doing what was done in English a few centuries ago.

Forming the Present Perfect with *sein*

You already know the conjugation of *sein*. Combine that verb with a past participle and you've got the present perfect tense with *sein*.

But hold on! You can't just use any old verb with the auxiliary verb *sein* and a past participle and be correct. *Sein* is used only with verbs of motion or verbs that express "existence" or "radical change." That may sound fancy, but it's not so complicated.

- Verbs of motion show direction or movement from one place to another: *gehen* (to go), *fahren* (to drive), *fliegen* (to fly), *kommen* (to come), *laufen* (to run), *fallen* (to fall), *reisen* (to travel).
- Verbs of existence or radical change are those that you can't control. They describe things that happen "to you" without your doing anything: *sein* (to be), *werden* (to become), *bleiben* (to stay), *sterben* (to die), *geschehen* (to occur, happen), *passieren* (to happen).

You can test a verb to see if it fits into one of the above two categories that require *sein*. Pretend your feet are glued to the floor. Then give yourself a command with a verb. If you can carry out the action without moving your feet, the verb will most likely use *haben* as its auxiliary: Sing! Laugh! Read! Eat! Buy! Speak! Ask!

If the command requires you to move your feet from one place to another to carry out the action, the verb will use *sein* as its auxiliary: Go! Run! Fly! Travel! Fall!

And if you have no control over the action because it's something that just occurs, the verb will use *sein* as its auxiliary as well: Be! Become! Stay! Die!

 Fact

Another way to decide whether a past participle uses *haben* or *sein* to form the present perfect is to check whether the verb can have a direct object. If it can, use *haben*. If it can't, use *sein*. *Er hat ein Buch gelesen.* (He read a book.) *Er ist in die Stadt gefahren.* (He drove to the city.)

Let's look at some examples of past participles that require *sein* as their auxiliary or helping verb.

▼ PAST PARTICIPLES WITH *SEIN*

Infinitive	Present Perfect Tense	English Meaning
bleiben	*ich bin geblieben*	I have stayed
fahren	*sie ist gefahren*	she has driven

Infinitive	Present Perfect Tense	English Meaning
fallen	Sie sind gefallen	you have fallen
gehen	er ist gegangen	he has gone
geschehen	es ist geschehen	it has occurred
kommen	du bist gekommen	you have come
laufen	wir sind gelaufen	we have run
passieren	es ist passiert	it has happened
reisen	ihr seid gereist	you all have traveled
sein	ich bin gewesen	I have been
sterben	er ist gestorben	he has died
werden	sie ist geworden	she has become

Note that past participles of verbs whose infinitives end in *–ieren* do not take the prefix *ge–*: *Er hat studiert.* (He studied.) *Es ist passiert.* (It happened.)

Exercise 14-2

Decide whether the verbs should be used with *sein* or *haben* in the present perfect tense and form the past participle with the subject provided. For example, when presented with the words *er/sagen*, you say, *Er hat gesagt.*

1. *ich/fragen* _____
2. *sie* (pl.)*/reisen* _____
3. *du/sehen* _____
4. *wir/finden* _____
5. *ihr/sein* _____
6. *ich/bleiben* _____
7. *wir/wissen* _____
8. *du/stören* _____
9. *er/essen* _____
10. *sie* (pl.)*/kommen* _____
11. *du/stellen* _____
12. *Sie/gehen* _____
13. *ich/laufen* _____

14. *er/sterben*_____

15. *wir/nehmen* _____

The Past Perfect Tense

German has the same tenses as English, and the past perfect tense is the next one to consider. The past perfect is formed the same way as the present perfect tense, except that the auxiliary verb is conjugated in the past tense when it is combined with a past participle.

In English, for example, in the present perfect tense you say, "I have repaired the car." In the past perfect tense you say, "I had repaired the car." Naturally, we have to be aware of the second tense formation in English: "I had been repairing the car." That form doesn't exist in German.

German has two auxiliary verbs in the perfect tenses: *haben* and *sein*. Verbs that take direct objects usually use *haben* as their auxiliary: *Er hat es gefunden.* (He found it.) *Wir haben den Mann gesehen.* (We saw the man.) Verbs of motion and those that express existence or a radical change use *sein*: *Er ist in die Stadt gefahren.* (He drove to the city.) *Wir sind zu Hause geblieben.* (We stayed at home.) *Sie ist gestorben.* (She died.)

In the past perfect tense, you use the past tense of the helping verb, so *haben* becomes *hatten* and *sein* becomes *waren*: *Er hatte es gefunden.* (He had found it.) *Er war in die Stadt gefahren.* (He had driven to the city.)

Conjugated past tense form of *haben* or *sein* + past participle = past perfect tense

Take a look at the complete conjugation of both types of participles.

▼ **THE PAST PERFECT TENSE**

haben	sein
ich hatte gelacht	ich war gegangen
(I had laughed)	(I had traveled)
du hattest gesehen	du warst geblieben
(you had seen)	(you had stayed)

haben	sein
er/sie/es hatte gefunden	er/sie/es war gekommen
(he/she/it had found)	(he/she/it had come)
wir hatten gespielt	wir waren geflogen
(we had played)	(we had flown)
ihr hattet gesungen	ihr wart gewesen
(you all had sung)	(you all had been)
Sie hatten gemacht	Sie waren geworden
(you had done)	(you had become)
sie (pl.) hatten gehört	sie waren gelaufen
(they had heard)	(they had run)

 Question

How is the past perfect different from the past tense?
The past perfect tense allows you to distinguish between two events that happened at different times in the past. "I washed the dishes after I had eaten dinner." Both eating and washing took place in the past, but eating dinner was further in the past.

The past perfect tense differs from the present perfect tense in that it tells of an action that began in the past and ended in the past. The German present perfect tense is most often used where the simple past is used in English: *Er hat Deutsch gesprochen.* (He spoke German.) *Sie ist nach Hause gegangen.* (She went home.) But if you say in the past perfect tense, "He had spoken German as a child," you infer that he did speak German when he was young, but for some reason that ended in the past and he doesn't speak German anymore. The same concept applies in German. (Be aware, however, that German often uses the present tense where the present perfect would be used in English.)

Present Perfect Structure:

Er hat seit seiner Kindheit Deutsch gesprochen.
(He has spoken German since his childhood.)

Present Tense Structure with the same English translation:

Er spricht seit seiner Kindheit Deutsch.
(He has spoken German since his childhood.)

Past Perfect Structure:

Er hatte als Kind Deutsch gesprochen.
(He had spoken German as a child.)

Exercise 14-3

Restate the sentences below in the past perfect tense. Watch for verbs that use *sein* rather than *haben* as the auxiliary.

1. *Hans und Maria laufen in den Garten.* (Hans and Maria run into the garden.)

   _____

2. *Ich bekomme einen Brief von Helga.* (I receive a letter from Helga.)

   _____

3. *Wer repariert den Wagen?* (Who is repairing the car?)

   _____

4. *Er fragt mich* (He asks me.)

   _____

5. *Ich trinke ein Glas Wasser.* (I am drinking a glass of water.)

   _____

6. *Wer kennt die Frau?* (Who knows the woman?)

   _____

7. *Wir reisen nach Berlin.* (We travel to Berlin.)

   _____

8. *Liest du das Buch?* (Are you reading the book?)

   _____

9. *Er trägt einen Hut.* (He wears a hat.)

   _____

10. *Ich bleibe zu Hause.* (I stay home.)

   _____

The Future Perfect Tense

As in other "perfect" tenses, a past participle is part of the formation of the future perfect tense. The auxiliary verb that is used for this tense is *werden*. It is followed at the end of the sentence by a past participle and then either *haben* or *sein*.

Conjugated form of *werden* + past participle + *haben* or *sein* = future perfect tense

Recall that verbs that take direct objects usually use *haben* as their auxiliary. Verbs of motion and those that express existence or a radical change use *sein*. The same verbs that form the present perfect and past perfect with *sein* also form the future perfect with *sein* as their auxiliary verb:

Er wird es gefunden haben.	He will have found it.
Wir werden den Mann gesehen haben.	We will have seen the man.
Er wird in die Stadt gefahren sein.	He will have driven to the city.
Wir werden zu Hause geblieben sein.	We will have stayed at home.
Sie wird weggegangen sein.	She will have gone out.

The meaning of this tense is "will have done" something.

▼ THE FUTURE PERFECT TENSE

German Phrase	English Meaning
ich werde gesucht haben	I will have looked for
du wirst gesehen haben	you will have seen
er/sie/es wird gemacht haben	he/she/it will have made
wir werden gewesen sein	we will have been
ihr werdet gegangen sein	you will have gone
Sie werden geworden sein	you will have become
sie (pl.) *werden besucht haben*	they will have visited

This tense is used to show an action that will be completed in the future. But just as the present tense can infer a future meaning, the present perfect tense can infer a future perfect meaning.

Er fliegt morgen nach Hause.
He will fly home tomorrow.

Bis ich an die Ecke komme, ist der Bus bestimmt schon abgefahren.
By the time I get to the corner, the bus will surely have departed.

There is a tendency to use the simpler version of the future and future perfect tenses, especially in conversational German.

The perfect tenses are so named because they have a past participle in their structure. The differences among the three perfect tenses arise from the tense of the auxiliary verb used. In the present perfect tense, the auxiliary is a present tense conjugation of *haben* or *sein*. In the past perfect tense, the auxiliary is a past tense conjugation of *haben* or *sein*. And in the future perfect tense, the conjugated auxiliary is *werden*. But all three auxiliaries are accompanied by a past participle—either regular or irregular.

Exercise 14-4

Restate each present tense phrase in the present perfect, the past perfect, and the future perfect. For example:

			ich werde
ich lerne	ich habe gelernt	ich hatte gelernt	gelernt haben
1. *er schlägt*			
2. *sie* (pl.) *bringen*			
3. *es passiert*			
4. *sie* (sing.) *ist*			
5. *du hast*			
6. *ihr esst*			
7. *Sie kommen*			
8. *wer reist*			

9. *wir setzen* ＿＿＿＿＿＿＿ ＿＿＿＿＿＿＿ ＿＿＿＿＿＿＿

10. *ich sehe* ＿＿＿＿＿＿＿ ＿＿＿＿＿＿＿ ＿＿＿＿＿＿＿

 ## Question

> **How is *werden* different when it means "to become" or "to get" and when it means "will" or "shall?"**
>
> When *werden* stands alone in a sentence, it means "become" or "get," for example: *Es wird sehr kalt.* (It is becoming very cold.) When *werden* is followed by an infinitive or a past participle accompanied by *haben* or *sein*, it is the future tense auxiliary, for example: *Er wird Bonn besuchen* (He will visit Bonn) or *Er wird Bonn besucht haben* (He will have visited Bonn).

The Spoken Past Versus the Written Past

Now that you have been introduced to all the tenses, it's time to make something quite clear: German speakers tend to use the present perfect tense as the preferred tense to express something that occurred in the past. They might switch to the simple past when narrating an event. The simple past, however, tends to be preferred in written German. Let's look at some examples.

▼ **SPOKEN PAST VERSUS THE WRITTEN PAST**

Spoken German	Written German	English
Er ist zu Hause geblieben.	*Er blieb zu Hause.*	He stayed home.
Ich habe es gehört.	*Ich hörte es.*	I heard it.
Haben Sie es verstanden?	*Verstanden Sie es?*	Did you understand it?

CHAPTER 15

Should I or Shouldn't I?

Y ou've learned a lot of verbs by now. This chapter covers some special verbs that act a little differently from the ones you already know. Modal auxiliary verbs let you modify a phrase, and you'll find them used quite frequently in German. The following sections also look at verbs with prefixes and the forms they take in other tenses.

What Is a Modal Auxiliary?

In both English and German there are certain words that put "emotion" or "a special spin" on a sentence. They're often called auxiliaries or helping verbs.

Such words convey that you *want* to do something or that you *must* do something, for example. To generalize, you can say that they express permission, obligation, wish, desire, and possibility. The German verbs of this type are called modal auxiliaries. The meaning of a sentence is altered by the addition of a modal auxiliary. To use them, you conjugate them and follow them with an infinitive at the end of the sentence. One such modal auxiliary is *sollen* (should, ought to). In a sentence, it looks like this: *Er soll ihm einen Brief schreiben.* (He should write him a letter.) Did you notice the infinitive at the very end of the sentence?

There are six modal auxiliaries in German. In the following tables they are shown conjugated in the present tense. Their infinitives and meaning are: *dürfen* (may, to be allowed to), *können* (can, to be able to), *mögen* (to like), *müssen* (must, to have to), *sollen* (should, ought to), and *wollen* (to want). Notice the irregularity of the forms for *ich, du, er, sie,* and *es.*

▼ PRESENT TENSE OF *DÜRFEN* (MAY, TO BE ALLOWED TO)

Person	Conjugation	Person	Conjugation
First (sing.)	*ich darf*	First (pl.)	*wir dürfen*
Second (sing.)	*du darfst*	Second (pl.)	*ihr dürft*
		Second (formal)	*Sie dürfen*
Third (sing.)	*er/sie/es darf*	Third (pl.)	*sie dürfen*

▼ PRESENT TENSE OF *KÖNNEN* (CAN, TO BE ABLE TO)

Person	Conjugation	Person	Conjugation
First (sing.)	*ich kann*	First (pl.)	*wir können*
Second (sing.)	*du kannst*	Second (pl.)	*ihr könnt*
		Second (formal)	*Sie können*
Third (sing.)	*er/sie/es kann*	Third (pl.)	*sie können*

▼ PRESENT TENSE OF *MÖGEN* (TO LIKE)

Person	Conjugation	Person	Conjugation
First (sing.)	*ich mag*	First (pl.)	*wir mögen*
Second (sing.)	*du magst*	Second (pl.)	*ihr mögt*
		Second (formal)	*Sie mögen*
Third (sing.)	*er/sie/es mag*	Third (pl.)	*sie mögen*

▼ PRESENT TENSE OF *MÜSSEN* (MUST, TO HAVE TO)

Person	Conjugation	Person	Conjugation
First (sing.)	*ich muss*	First (pl.)	*wir müssen*
Second (sing.)	*du musst*	Second (pl.)	*ihr müsst*
		Second (formal)	*Sie müssen*
Third (sing.)	*er/sie/es muss*	Third (pl.)	*sie müssen*

▼ PRESENT TENSE OF *SOLLEN* (SHOULD, OUGHT TO)

Person	Conjugation	Person	Conjugation
First (sing.)	*ich soll*	First (pl.)	*wir sollen*
Second (sing.)	*du sollst*	Second (pl.)	*ihr sollt*
		Second (formal)	*Sie sollen*
Third (sing.)	*er/sie/es soll*	Third (pl.)	*sie sollen*

▼ PRESENT TENSE OF *WOLLEN* (TO WANT)

Person	Conjugation	Person	Conjugation
First (sing.)	*ich will*	First (pl.)	*wir wollen*
Second (sing.)	*du willst*	Second (pl.)	*ihr wollt*
		Second (formal)	*Sie wollen*
Third (sing.)	*er/sie/es will*	Third (pl.)	*sie wollen*

Er besucht seinen Onkel.	He visits his uncle.
Er darf seinen Onkel besuchen.	He may visit his uncle.
Er kann seinen Onkel besuchen.	He can visit his uncle.
Er muss seinen Onkel besuchen.	He has to visit his uncle.
Er soll seinen Onkel besuchen.	He should visit his uncle.
Er will seinen Onkel besuchen.	He wants to visit his uncle.

One of the keys to accuracy is to remember to place the infinitive at the end of the sentence: *Er will seinen Onkel besuchen.*

Watch out for *können* and *mögen!* The modal auxiliary *können* has a special function. It's used alone in a sentence to infer that someone knows a language and that he or she can read, write, speak, and understand that language. For example: *Er kann Deutsch.* (He knows German. In other words, he can read, write, speak, and understand German.) A few more examples:

Können Sie Englisch?	Do you speak English?
Kann Helga Spanisch?	Can Helga understand Spanish?
Ich kann Russisch.	I speak Russian.

The modal auxiliary *mögen* tends to be used most often in its subjunctive form, *möchten* (would like): *Ich möchte in Berlin bleiben.* (I'd like to stay in Berlin.)

Modals in the Past

In the past tense, the modal auxiliaries follow the pattern of regular verbs. If the infinitive of the modal verb has an umlaut, however, the umlaut is omitted throughout the past tense conjugation.

▼ **THE PAST TENSE OF *DÜRFEN***

Person	Conjugation	Person	Conjugation
First (sing.)	*ich durfte*	First (pl.)	*wir durften*
Second (sing.)	*du durftest*	Second (pl.)	*ihr durftet*
		Second (formal)	*Sie durften*
Third (sing.)	*er/sie/es durfte*	Third (pl.)	*sie durften*

▼ **THE PAST TENSE OF *KÖNNEN***

Person	Conjugation	Person	Conjugation
First (sing.)	*ich konnte*	First (pl.)	*wir konnten*
Second (sing.)	*du konntest*	Second (pl.)	*ihr konntet*
		Second (formal)	*Sie konnten*
Third (sing.)	*er/sie/es konnte*	Third (pl.)	*sie konnten*

▼ **THE PAST TENSE OF *MÖGEN***

Person	Conjugation	Person	Conjugation
First (sing.)	*ich mochte*	First (pl.)	*wir mochten*
Second (sing.)	*du mochtest*	Second (pl.)	*ihr mochtet*
		Second (formal)	*Sie mochten*
Third (sing.)	*er/sie/es mochte*	Third (pl.)	*sie mochten*

▼ THE PAST TENSE OF *MÜSSEN*

Person	Conjugation	Person	Conjugation
First (sing.)	*ich musste*	First (pl.)	*wir mussten*
Second (sing.)	*du musstest*	Second (pl.)	*ihr musstet*
		Second (formal)	*Sie mussten*
Third (sing.)	*er/sie/es musste*	Third (pl.)	*sie mussten*

▼ THE PAST TENSE OF *SOLLEN*

Person	Conjugation	Person	Conjugation
First (sing.)	*ich sollte*	First (pl.)	*wir sollten*
Second (sing.)	*du solltest*	Second (pl.)	*ihr solltet*
		Second (formal)	*Sie sollten*
Third (sing.)	*er/sie/es sollte*	Third (pl.)	*sie sollten*

▼ THE PAST TENSE OF *WOLLEN*

Person	Conjugation	Person	Conjugation
First (sing.)	*ich wollte*	First (pl.)	*wir wollten*
Second (sing.)	*du wolltest*	Second (pl.)	*ihr wolltet*
		Second (formal)	*Sie wollten*
Third (sing.)	*er/sie/es wollte*	Third (pl.)	*sie wollten*

By using the past tense conjugation of the modal auxiliary, you change the meaning of the sentence to the past:

Er musste seinen Onkel besuchen.   He had to visit his uncle.
Er wollte seinen Onkel besuchen.   He wanted to visit his uncle.

Notice how the past tense meaning of the modals is different from the present tense meaning.

dürfen: ich darf (I may) / *ich durfte* (I was allowed)
können: ich kann (I can) / *ich konnte* (I could, was able to)
mögen: ich mag (I like) / *ich mochte* (I liked)
müssen: ich muss (I must, I have to) / *ich musste* (I had to)

sollen: ich soll (I should, I ought to) / *ich sollte* (I should have, I ought to have)

wollen: ich will (I want) / *ich wollte* (I wanted)

The modal auxiliary *mögen* tends to be used most often in its subjunctive form *möchten* (would like): *Er möchte seine Tante besuchen.* (He would like to visit his aunt.)

Don't confuse *mochte* and *möchte*. *Mochte* is the past tense of *mögen* and means "liked." *Möchte* (with an umlaut) is a polite way of saying "would like."

Forming the Present Perfect Tense

You've been using modal auxiliaries in the present and past tenses. Now it's time to look at them in the present perfect tense and the future tense. They do something special in those tenses, but it's nothing to get nervous about. All of the modal auxiliaries use *haben* in the present perfect tense. And they all form their participles like regular verbs, using the *ge–* prefix and *–t* suffix.

If the modal is the only verb in the sentence, you can conjugate it in the present perfect tense just like a regular verb. For example: *Ich kann es nicht* (I am not able to) becomes *Ich habe es nicht gekonnt* (I was not able to). The modal past participles look like this:

dürfen	*haben gedurft*	*müssen*	*haben gemusst*
können	*haben gekonnt*	*sollen*	*haben gesollt*
mögen	*haben gemocht*	*wollen*	*haben gewollt*

But modal auxiliaries are used much more often with other verbs: *Ich will meinem Bruder helfen.* (I want to help my brother.) *Kannst du mir einen Bleistift geben?* (Can you give me a pencil?) *Die Kinder müssen jetzt nach Hause gehen.* (The children must go home now.) When the modals are used in sentences with other verbs, the present perfect tense is formed differently. The modal is not formed as a participle, but remains an infinitive and is placed behind the other verb at the very end of the sentence. This is called a double infinitive structure. This is how it looks.

Sie hat nicht mitkommen dürfen.
She has not been permitted to come along.

Wir haben es nicht verstehen können.
We haven't been able to understand it.

Ich habe meinem Bruder helfen müssen.
I have had to help my brother.

Die Kinder haben im Garten spielen wollen.
The children have wanted to play in the garden.

Ich habe nicht mitgehen können.
I wasn't able to go along.

Exercise 15-1

Restate the following present tense sentences in the present perfect tense.

1. *Musst du zu Hause bleiben?* (Do you have to stay at home?)

   _____

2. *Mein Vetter kann Klavier spielen.* (My cousin can play the piano.)

   _____

3. *Darf er mit deiner Frau tanzen?* (May he dance with your wife?)

   _____

4. *Der Lehrer soll lauter sprechen.* (The teacher should talk louder.)

   _____

5. *Wir wollen Brot mit Käse essen.* (We want to eat bread with cheese.)

   _____

6. *Ich muss viel arbeiten.* (I have to work a lot.)

   _____

7. *Die Jungen können Tennis spielen.* (The boys can play tennis.)

   _____

8. *Dürft ihr mit der Katze spielen?* (Are you allowed to play with the cat?)

___

9. *Die Männer sollen weniger Bier trinken.* (The men should drink less beer.)

___

10. *Will sie Karl kennen lernen?* (Does she want to meet Karl?)

___

 Alert

When a modal auxiliary is used in a double infinitive structure in the present perfect tense, its translation is usually stated in the simple past tense in order to avoid an awkward structure in English. For example, *Thomas hat Englisch lernen wollen.* (Thomas wanted to learn English.)

The Future of Modals

The same kind of double infinitive structure occurs when you form the future tense with modal verbs. You conjugate *werden* normally and place the modal auxiliary in infinitive form at the end of the sentence behind the other verb.

Sie wird nicht mitkommen dürfen.
She will not be permitted to come along.

Der Student wird es leicht verstehen können.
The student will easily be able to understand it.

Mein Bruder wird mir helfen müssen.
My brother will have to help me.

Die Kinder werden mit dem Hund spielen wollen.
The children will want to play with the dog.

Exercise 15-2

Restate the following present tense sentences in the future tense.

1. *Ich darf nicht zu Hause bleiben.* (I may not stay at home.)

   _____

2. *Diese Leute wollen mit dem Bus fahren.* (These people want to go by bus.)

   _____

3. *Warum muss ich auf ihn warten?* (Why do I have to wait for him?)

   _____

4. *Er kann schnell lernen.* (He can learn quickly.)

   _____

5. *Könnt ihr ihn verstehen?* (Can you all understand him?)

   _____

6. *Müssen Sie in Bonn bleiben?* (Do you have to stay in Bonn?)

   _____

7. *Erik will mit Tina tanzen.* (Erik wants to dance with Tina.)

   _____

8. *Kannst du lauter sprechen?* (Can you speak louder?)

   _____

9. *Sie darf nicht mitgehen.* (She's not allowed to go along.)

   _____

10. *Ihr wollt nicht mehr arbeiten.* (You don't want to work anymore.)

   _____

Another Look at Inseparable Prefixes

You've already learned that some German verbs take prefixes. German prefixes act much like English prefixes: They change the meaning of the verb. But German prefixes also change how a verb is conjugated.

With inseparable prefixes, the prefix cannot be separated from the verb. The inseparable prefixes are: *be–*, *ent–*, *emp–*, *er–*, *ge–*, *ver–*, and *zer–*. As you know, verbs with prefixes are closely related to the original verb; if the verb without a prefix is regular, any verbs formed by adding a prefix to it are also regular. Irregular verbs also remain irregular despite any prefix.

The main change that occurs when a verb has an inseparable prefix is its formation as a participle. You do not add the prefix *ge–* to a verb that has an inseparable prefix to form its participle. Let's look at some examples.

 Fact

Some prefixes, such as *unter* and *über*, can be either separable or inseparable. So how can you tell which they are? If the prefix is stressed in the pronunciation of a verb (as in the verb *úntergehen* [to sink]), it is separable. But if the stress is not on the prefix, as in the verbs *unternéhmen* (to undertake) and *übersétzen* (to translate), the prefix is inseparable.

▼ **VERBS WITH AND WITHOUT INSEPARABLE PREFIXES**

Tense	Verb with No Prefix	Verb with Inseparable Prefix
	kommen (to come)	*bekommen* (to receive)
Present	*ich komme*	*ich bekomme*
Past	*ich kam*	*ich bekam*
Future	*ich werde kommen*	*ich werde bekommen*
Pres. Perfect	*ich bin **ge**kommen*	*ich habe **be**kommen*
	warten (to wait)	*erwarten* (to expect)
Present	*er wartet*	*er erwartet*
Past	*er wartete*	*er erwartete*
Future	*er wird warten*	*er wird erwarten*
Pres. Perfect	*er hat **ge**wartet*	*er hat **er**wartet*
	stehen (to stand)	*verstehen* (to understand)
Present	*wir stehen*	*wir verstehen*
Past	*wir standen*	*wir verstanden*
Future	*wir werden stehen*	*wir werden verstehen*
Pres. Perfect	*wir haben **ge**standen*	*wir haben **ve**rstanden*

Revisiting the Separable Prefixes

Separable prefixes are removed from the infinitive when the verb is conjugated in the present and past tenses. And to form the past participle of a verb with a separable prefix, the prefix *ge–* is inserted between the separable prefix and the main part of the verb.

Forming the Simple Past and Future Tenses

You already learned how to conjugate a verb with a separable prefix in the present tense. You place the prefix at the end of the sentence and conjugate the verb normally. For example, the infinitive *ansehen* (to look at) looks like this when conjugated in the present tense:

Ich sehe . . . an.	*Wir sehen . . . an.*
Du siehst . . . an.	*Ihr seht . . . an.*
Er sieht . . . an.	*Sie sehen . . . an.*

In the past tense, the main part of the verb is conjugated the same way you already learned:

Ich sah . . . an.	*Wir sahen . . . an.*
Du sahst . . . an.	*Ihr saht . . . an.*
Er sah . . . an.	*Sie sahen . . . an.*

There are no new rules for forming the future tense. Just conjugate *werden* and place the entire infinitive at the end of the sentence. For example, the infinitive *aufstehen* (to get up) is conjugated in the first person as follows: *Ich werde . . . aufstehen.* The infinitive *ausgeben* (to spend) in the future looks like: *Er wird . . . ausgeben.*

Participles and Perfect Tenses

A past participle with a separable prefix is written as one word with the prefix *ge–* separating the prefix from the rest of the participle:

aufstehen (to get up)	*aufgestanden*
ausgeben (to spend)	*ausgegeben*

hinlegen (to put down, put away)   *hingelegt*
mitkommen (to come along)   *mitgekommen*

Let's look at some examples and the meanings derived from using separable prefixes.

▼ **VERBS WITH AND WITHOUT SEPARABLE PREFIXES**

Tense	Verb with No Prefix	Verb with Separable Prefix
	kommen (to come)	**mitkommen (to accompany)**
Present	*ich komme*	*ich komme mit*
Past	*ich kam*	*ich kam mit*
Future	*ich werde kommen*	*ich werde mitkommen*
Pres. Perfect	*ich bin gekommen*	*ich bin mitgekommen*
	bringen (to bring)	**beibringen (to teach)**
Present	*er bringt*	*er bringt bei*
Past	*er brachte*	*er brachte bei*
Future	*er wird bringen*	*er wird beibringen*
Pres. Perfect	*er hat gebracht*	*er hat beigebracht*
	legen (to lay, put)	**hinlegen (to put down, put away)**
Present	*wir legen*	*wir legen hin*
Past	*wir legten*	*wir legten hin*
Future	*wir werden legen*	*wir werden hinlegen*
Pres. Perfect	*wir haben gelegt*	*wir haben hingelegt*

Exercise 15-3

Restate the following infinitives with the pronoun *er* in the present perfect tense. For example:

singen (to sing)   <u>er hat gesungen</u>

1. *versprechen* (to promise) _____
2. *besuchen* (to visit) _____
3. *verstehen* (to understand) _____
4. *ausgeben* (to spend) _____
5. *verkaufen* (to sell) _____
6. *abfahren* (to depart) _____

7. *erwarten* (to expect)   _____

8. *erkennen* (to recognize)   _____

9. *bestellen* (to order)   _____

10. *bekommen* (to receive)   _____

CHAPTER 16

What's Mine Is Yours

How do you talk about something that belongs to you or to someone else? You need to know how to form the possessive. In this chapter you will learn how to talk about "your car," "John's friend," and "our school." And you'll meet the last case in German—the genitive case—which is often used when talking about possession.

What Belongs to You and Me

Just like English, German shows "to whom" something belongs by using a possessive adjective. *Mein* means "my" and *dein* means "your." The German possessive adjectives require endings that show gender—just like *ein* and *kein*. Look at these examples.

▼ GENDER WITH POSSESSIVE ADJECTIVES

Masculine Nouns	Feminine Nouns	Neuter Nouns	Plural Nouns
der Freund	die Schule	das Haus	die Freunde
ein Freund	eine Schule	ein Haus	zehn Freunde
kein Freund	keine Schule	kein Haus	keine Freunde
mein Freund	meine Schule	mein Haus	meine Freunde
dein Freund	deine Schule	dein Haus	deine Freunde

When masculine nouns are used as direct objects, the ending *–en* is required on the article, on *kein*, or on the possessive adjectives (*mein*, *dein): Ich sehe den Freund. Ich sehe einen Freund. Ich sehe keinen Freund. Ich sehe meinen Freund. Ich sehe deinen Freund.*

The Rest of the Possessive Adjectives

The possessive adjectives *mein* and *dein* were easy to pick up because they acted like *ein* and *kein* with nouns. But now it's time to learn the rest of the possessive adjectives. Just as *mein* refers to the pronoun *ich* and *dein* refers to the pronoun *du*, the remaining possessive adjectives refer to specific pronouns.

▼ **POSSESSIVE ADJECTIVES**

Pronoun	Possessive Adjective	English	Pronoun	Possessive Adjective	English
ich	*mein*	my	*wir*	*unser*	our
du	*dein*	your	*ihr*	*euer*	your
er	*sein*	his	*Sie*	*Ihr*	your
sie (sing.)	*ihr*	her	*sie* (pl.)	*ihr*	their
es	*sein*	its			

Masculine nouns will use *sein* as their possessive adjective, feminine nouns will use *ihr*, neuter nouns will use *sein*, and plural nouns will use *ihr*.

Der Mann findet sein Ticket.	The man finds his ticket.
Die Dame sieht ihren Sohn.	The lady sees her son.
Das Kind liebt seine Eltern.	The child loves his parents.
Die Kinder suchten ihre Bücher.	The children looked for their books.

Remember that your choice of which possessive adjective to use depends on the gender of the noun it represents, not on the noun it modifies. In the sentence *Die Dame sieht ihren Sohn*, the woman (*die Dame*) is feminine and therefore uses the possessive adjective *ihr* to mean "her." Her son (*der Sohn*) is masculine and the direct object, so the possessive adjective must take the masculine ending *–en*.

Just as certain endings are required with *ein, kein, mein,* and *dein,* the same endings are required for all possessive adjectives. These endings show gender and indicate masculine nouns in the accusative case. The endings for the feminine, neuter, and plural are identical in both the nominative and accusative cases.

The following list shows what the endings for possessive adjectives look like with nouns of different gender in the nominative case. (Remember that the nominative case is the case used when a noun is the subject of a sentence.)

Masculine Nouns	*mein Lehrer, dein Lehrer, sein Lehrer, ihr Lehrer, unser Lehrer, euer Lehrer, Ihr Lehrer, ihr Lehrer*
Feminine Nouns	*meine Lampe, deine Lampe, seine Lampe, ihre Lampe, unsere Lampe, eure Lampe, Ihre Lampe, ihre Lampe*
Neuter Nouns	*mein Buch, dein Buch, sein Buch, ihr Buch, unser Buch, euer Buch, Ihr Buch, ihr Buch*
Plural Nouns	*meine Hefte, deine Hefte, seine Hefte, ihre Hefte, unsere Hefte, eure Hefte, Ihre Hefte, ihre Hefte*

Now look at the endings used on the possessive adjectives in the accusative case. Recall that the accusative case is used when a noun is the direct object of a sentence, or following an accusative preposition.

Masculine Nouns	*meinen Lehrer, deinen Lehrer, seinen Lehrer, ihren Lehrer, unseren Lehrer, euren Lehrer, Ihren Lehrer, ihren Lehrer*
Feminine Nouns	*meine Lampe, deine Lampe, seine Lampe, ihre Lampe, unsere Lampe, eure Lampe, Ihre Lampe, ihre Lampe*
Neuter Nouns	*mein Buch, dein Buch, sein Buch, ihr Buch, unser Buch, euer Buch, Ihr Buch, ihr Buch*
Plural Nouns	*meine Hefte, deine Hefte, seine Hefte, ihre Hefte, unsere Hefte, eure Hefte, Ihre Hefte, ihre Hefte*

If you compare these two lists, you will see that the endings in both cases are the same for feminine, neuter, and plural nouns. It is only the masculine gender that takes different endings in the accusative case. Note that when you put an ending on *euer*, there is a slight change of spelling: *euer, euren, eure.*

Exercise 16-1

Using the pronouns, decide which possessive adjective to use to complete each sentence. For example, when presented with *ich / Sabine findet _____ Buch*, you write, *Sabine findet mein Buch.* Sabine finds my book, because *mein* is the possessive adjective form of *ich.* (Watch out for masculine words in the accusative case! You'll need an *–en* ending.)

1. *du / Vater war im Wohnzimmer.*

_____

2. *sie* (sing.) */ Ich kenne Mutter.*

_____

3. *er / Wir sahen Bruder im Theater.*

_____

4. *wir / Der Franzose kaufte Volkswagen.*

_____

5. *Sie / Wo ist Vetter?*

_____

6. *ich / Das sind Bücher.*

_____

7. *sie* (pl.) */ Wo ist Haus?*

_____

8. *ihr / Sind Plätze gut?*

_____

9. *er / Karl besuchte Onkel in der Hauptstadt.*

_____

10. *wir / Das ist ein Geschenk für Lehrerin.*

_____

A New Case

You're about to meet the fourth and final case in the German language. It's called the genitive case and it has a couple of simple and clear-cut functions. The primary use of the genitive case is to show possession. This is done in English with an apostrophe *s* (*–'s*) or the preposition "of":

- John's mother is a doctor.
- The roar of the lion sent shivers down his spine.

German also has the form that uses an *–s* to show possession, but you don't need an apostrophe. It's used primarily with names or descriptions of people that don't require an article:

Herberts Vater	Herbert's father
Mutters Bruder	Mother's brother
Mozarts Klaviermusik	Mozart's piano music

The most common form used to show possession involves the use of the genitive case. A genitive article is used to indicate possession. The genitive articles are shown in the following table.

▼ GENITIVE ARTICLES

Masculine	Feminine	Neuter	Plural
des	*der*	*des*	*der*
eines	*einer*	*eines*	*keiner*

Masculine and neuter nouns also require an *–s* ending to be added to the noun in the genitive case. If the noun has only one syllable, the ending is *–es* (*des Mannes*). If the noun has more than one syllable, the ending is *–s* (*des Lehrers*). Adjectives that describe a noun in the genitive also take an ending, but it's easy to remember because it is always *–en*.

▼ **GENITIVE ENDINGS**

Masculine	Feminine	Neuter	Plural
des netten Mannes	der netten Frau	des netten Kindes	der netten Kinder
eines netten Mannes	einer netten Frau	eines netten Kindes	keiner netten Kinder
Ihres netten Mannes	Ihrer netten Frau	Ihres netten Kindes	Ihrer netten Kinder

These phrases mean: "the nice man's / of the nice man," "the nice woman's / of the nice woman," "the nice child's / of the nice child," "the nice children's / of the nice children." Here are some examples of sentences that use the genitive case.

Die Tochter des netten Mannes ist Lehrerin.
The nice man's daughter is a teacher. / The daughter of the nice man is a teacher.

Ist der Hut Ihrer Frau hier im Esszimmer?
Is your wife's hat here in the dining room?

Die Stimme eines Kindes ist immer süß.
A child's voice is always sweet. / The voice of a child is always sweet.

Das Schlafzimmer meiner Kinder ist zu klein.
My children's bedroom is too little.

Wessen is the question word used to ask whose something is. *Wessen Haus ist das?* (Whose house is that?) The answer could be *Das ist das Haus unseres Vaters.* (That's our father's house.)

More Uses of the Genitive

There are four prepositions that require the genitive case after them. Interestingly, three of them have the concept of possession, because they use the word "of" to express their meaning.

▼ PREPOSITIONS THAT TAKE THE GENITIVE CASE

German	English	German	English
anstatt	instead of	*während*	during
trotz	in spite of	*wegen*	because of

Look how these four genitive prepositions are used in sentences.

Anstatt meiner Schwester ging Andreas in die Stadt.
Instead of my sister, Andreas went into the city.

Anstatt eines Freundes kam unser Onkel zu Besuch.
Instead of a friend, our uncle came for a visit.

Trotz des Regens blieb er nicht zu Hause.
In spite of the rain he didn't stay home.

Trotz des schönen Wetters bleibt er zu Hause.
In spite of the nice weather he stays at home.

Während des Tages arbeitet meine Nichte in einem Café.
During the day my niece works in a café.

Während des Krieges war ich in Schweden.
During the war I was in Sweden.

Wegen seiner Erkältung musste er zu Hause bleiben.
Because of his cold he had to stay home.

Wegen einer Prüfung gehen sie nicht ins Kino.
Because of a test they're not going to the movies.

CHAPTER 17

The Good, the Bad, and the Ugly

Adjectives modify and describe nouns, and you've encountered quite a few of them in German already. In German, adjectives reflect the gender, case, and number of the nouns they modify. In this chapter you'll learn more about using adjectives with the proper endings.

Antonyms and Other Words of Contrast

Pairs of words that show a contrast are helpful when giving an opinion about something. Is it good or is it bad? Was the play boring or interesting? Did you eat too much or too little roast beef?

The following pairs of words are antonyms, or words that show a strong contrast.

▼ WORDS OF CONTRAST

English Pair	German Pair	English Pair	German Pair
beautiful/ugly	hübsch/hässlich	fast/slow	schnell/langsam
big/little	groß/klein	funny/sad	lustig/traurig
black/white	schwarz/weiß	here/there	hier/da (or dort)
boring/interesting	langweilig/interessant	high/low	hoch/niedrig
cold/hot	kalt/heiß	hungry/full	hungrig/satt
dark/bright	dunkel/hell	lazy/diligent	faul/fleißig
dry/wet	trocken/nass	long/short	lang/kurz

English Pair	German Pair	English Pair	German Pair
fashionable/old-fashioned	*modisch/ altmodisch*	to break/to repair	*brechen/ reparieren*
a lot/a little	*viel/wenig*	to find/to lose	*finden/verlieren*
male/female	*männlich/ weiblich*	to give/to take	*geben/nehmen*
near/far	*nah/weit*	to laugh/to cry	*lachen/weinen*
old/new	*alt/neu*	to live/to die	*leben/sterben*
old/young	*alt/jung*	to love/to hate	*lieben/hassen*
smart/stupid	*klug/dumm*	to marry/to divorce	*heiraten/scheiden*
smooth/rough	*glatt/rauh*	to shout/to whisper	*schreien/flüstern*
to ask/to answer	*fragen/antworten*	to sit/to stand	*sitzen/stehen*

 Alert

Watch out! If you look in a dictionary, you'll find that "full" can be translated as *voll*. That's quite true, but in that case it's the opposite of "empty" (*leer*). If you use the word *voll* to mean the opposite of "hungry," you may say something you don't mean. *Ich bin satt* means "I am full (not hungry)." But *Ich bin voll* means "I'm drunk" or "I'm wasted."

Exercise 17-1

Complete each sentence with the appropriate antonym or contrasting word.

1. *Das Haus ist nicht klein, sondern* _____ .
   (The house isn't little but . . .)

2. *Dieses Bild ist nicht hässlich, sondern* _____ .
   (This picture isn't ugly but . . .)

3. *Die Suppe ist nicht kalt, sondern* _____ .
   (The soup isn't cold but . . .)

4. *Oma ist nicht jung, sondern* _____ .
   (Granny isn't young but . . .)

5. *Ich hasse Karl nicht. Ich* _____ *ihn.*
   (I don't hate Karl. I . . . him.)

6. *Er hat nicht viel Geld, sondern* _____ *Geld.*
   (He doesn't have a lot of money but . . . money)

7. *Der Film ist nicht lustig, sondern* _____ .
   (The movie isn't funny but . . .)

8. *Es ist nicht weiß, sondern* _____ .
   (It's not white but . . .)

9. *Der Schüler ist nicht dumm, sondern* _____ .
   (The pupil isn't stupid but . . .)

10. *Der Zug fährt nicht langsam, sondern* _____ .
    (The train isn't slow but . . .)

Practice using these words in sentences you already know. They'll come in very handy. To use any of the adjectives above in a simple sentence is easy: *Vater ist hungrig.* (Father is hungry.) However, if you place an adjective before a noun, it will require an ending, depending on the case and gender of the noun it is modifying: *Der hungrige Mann ist sehr krank.* (The hungry man is very sick.) Before you can figure out what adjective ending a word takes, you have to understand the difference between two types of identifying adjectives—*der* words and *ein* words.

There are two ways of saying that you're hungry: *ich bin hungrig* and *ich habe Hunger.* With the former, you conjugate *sein* with the adjective *hungrig* (literally, "I am hungry"). With the latter, you conjugate *haben* and follow it with the noun *Hunger* (literally, "I have hunger").

Der Words and ein Words

Der words are the definite articles (*der, die, das*) and any other adjectives that act like definite articles with nouns. They are called demonstrative adjectives.

▼ **DER** WORDS

dieser (this)	*jener* (that)	*solcher* (such)
jeder (each)	*mancher* (many a)	*welcher* (which)

You already know the ein words: *ein, kein, mein, dein, sein, ihr, unser, euer, Ihr,* and *ihr.* You need to compare these two groups of words in order to use adjective endings more accurately. To generalize, you can say that the most common adjective ending in German is *–en.* But when is an adjective ending something other than *–en?*

Der Words

The nominative case (subject of the sentence) is the critical area. In this case, the gender of the noun has to be specified. When you use a definite article, that becomes quite clear: *der Lehrer, die Lehrerin, das Kind.* And when you use an adjective with the definite articles, it always has an *–e* ending in the nominative: *der gute Lehrer* (the good teacher), *die nette Lehrerin* (the nice teacher), *das intelligente Kind* (the intelligent child).

No matter which *der* word you use, the adjective ending will always be just an *–e* in the nominative case.

▼ **DER** WORDS IN THE NOMINATIVE CASE

Masculine	Feminine	Neuter
dieser alte Mann	*diese alte Frau*	*dieses nette Kind*
this old man	this old woman	this nice child
jeder blaue Teller	*jede blaue Tasse*	*jedes blaue Glas*
each blue plate	each blue cup	each blue glass
jener junge Lehrer	*jene junge Lehrerin*	*jenes hübsche Mädchen*
that young teacher	that young teacher	that pretty girl
mancher gute Mann	*manche gute Frau*	*manches gute Kind*

Masculine	Feminine	Neuter
many a good man	many a good woman	many a good child
welcher neue Wagen	*welche neue Lampe*	*welches neue Fahrrad*
which new car	which new lamp	which new bicycle

Since the feminine and neuter are identical in the nominative and accusative cases, you can assume that the same endings will apply in the accusative.

Ein Words

With *ein* words, gender is shown as an adjective ending, rather than by the article. The final sound of the definite article (*der*, *die*, *das*) appears as the adjective ending: *ein guter Mann*, *eine gute Frau*, *ein gutes Kind*. Take a look at some further examples.

▼ *EIN* WORDS IN THE NOMINATIVE CASE

Masculine	Feminine	Neuter
kein alter Lehrer	*keine alte Lehrerin*	*kein nettes Kind*
no old teacher	no old teacher	no nice child
sein neuer Wagen	*seine neue Lampe*	*sein neues Haus*
his new car	his new lamp	his new house
unser junger Freund	*unsere junge Freundin*	*unser altes Buch*
our young friend	our young friend	our old book
Ihr roter Hut	*Ihre rote Jacke*	*Ihr rotes Hemd*
your red hat	your red jacket	your red shirt

Again, the feminine and neuter would be identical in the accusative case.

If you understand the idea that gender is shown in the *der* word when *der* words are used but is shown in the adjective when *ein* words are used, then you have a good grasp of German adjective endings. All other adjectives that follow *der* or *ein* words will end in *–en*.

Case	Masculine	Feminine	Neuter	Plural
Nom.	dieser nette Freund	diese nette Freundin	dieses nette Kind	diese netten Kinder
Nom.	sein netter Freund	seine nette Freundin	sein nettes Kind	seine netten Kinder
Acc.	diesen netten Freund	diese nette Freundin	dieses nette Kind	diese netten Kinder
Acc.	seinen netten Freund	seine nette Freundin	sein nettes Kind	seine netten Kinder
Dat.	diesem netten Freund	dieser netten Freundin	diesem netten Kind	diesen netten Kindern
Dat.	seinem netten Freund	seiner netten Freundin	seinem netten Kind	seinen netten Kindern
Gen.	dieses netten Freundes	dieser netten Freundin	dieses netten Kindes	dieser netten Kinder
Gen.	seines netten Freundes	seiner netten Freundin	seines netten Kindes	seiner netten Kinder

Adjectives of plural nouns, whether used with *der* words or *ein* words, have an *–en* ending in all cases: nominative, accusative, dative, and genitive.

Some Special Nouns

Certain masculine nouns do their own thing in the four cases. They tend to be a few old German words (*der Herr* [man], *der Mensch* [human]), words that were assimilated into German from other cultures with the accent on the last syllable (*der Sol**dat*** [soldier], *der Stu**dent*** [student]), or masculine nouns that end in *–e* (*der Junge* [boy], *der Löwe* [lion]). What's unique about this group of masculine nouns is that they all form their plural by adding an *–n* or *–en*: *die Herren, die Soldaten, die Jungen*.

Here's the novel part: They also add an *–n* or *–en* ending throughout the accusative, dative, and genitive cases. But unlike other masculine nouns in the genitive case, the nouns in this category do not end in *–s*.

▼ SPECIAL MASCULINE NOUNS

Case	Herr	Mensch	Soldat	Löwe
Nom.	der Herr	kein Mensch	dieser Soldat	ein Löwe
Acc.	den Herrn	keinen Menschen	diesen Soldaten	einen Löwen
Dat.	dem Herrn	keinem Menschen	diesem Soldaten	einem Löwen
Gen.	des Herrn	keines Menschen	dieses Soldaten	eines Löwen

Naturally, even with these special endings, these nouns function in sentences like any other masculine nouns.

Der Herr an der Ecke ist ein Freund von mir.	The man on the corner is a friend of mine.
Monika liebt diesen Soldaten.	Monika loves this soldier.
Was gibst du dem Löwen?	What do you give the lion?

Exercise 17-2

Fill in the blanks with the correct form of the adjectives shown in parentheses.

1. *(neu) Wie viel kostet ein _____ Wagen?* (How much does a new car cost?)
2. *(hässlich) Eine _____ Katze steht vor der Tür.* (An ugly cat is standing in front of the door.)
3. *(interessant) Das ist ein _____ Roman.* (That is an interesting novel.)
4. *(deutsch) Der _____ Rennwagen ist sehr schnell.* (The German racecar is very fast.)
5. *(weiß) Dein _____ Kleid ist zu kurz.* (Your white dress is too short.)
6. *(braun) Ich habe einen _____ Hund.* (I have a brown dog.)
7. *(schön) Sie trägt eine _____ Jacke.* (She's wearing a pretty jacket.)
8. *(neu) Meine _____ Freunde sind in Köln.* (My new friends are in Cologne.)

9. (*alt*) *Kennst du diese* _____ *Frau?* (Do you know this old woman?)

10. (*jung*) *Ein* _____ *Mann wartet auf uns.* (A young man waits for us.)

Making Comparisons

When you use an adjective, you make a judgment or give an opinion about size, color, or quality: the big tree, a yellow rose, a distinguished gentleman. But when you want to compare two persons or things, you have to know the comparative form of the adjective. That's not as complicated as it sounds. When you make a judgment or express an opinion using a comparative adjective, you decide which of two things has more or less of the quality in question. And you use "than" as the word that divides the comparison:

tall: John is taller than Mary.
rich: My parents are richer than your parents.
green: The grass is greener here than on the other side of the fence.
interesting: This novel is more interesting than that novel.

Forming English comparative adjectives is relatively easy: just add *–er* to the adjective. There are a few spelling rules to keep in mind, but in general, most comparative adjectives follow the same pattern:

big/bigger	poor/poorer	kind/kinder
funny/funnier	silly/sillier	

But longer adjectives—adjectives that come to English from a Latin source—do not add *–er* to form the comparative. Instead, you place the word "more" in front of the adjective:

interesting/more interesting
superficial/more superficial
responsible/more responsible

English also has a few irregular comparative forms:

good/better   much/more

bad/worse   many/more

German is much the same. The comparative of most adjectives is formed by adding –er to the adjective.

▼ **COMPARATIVE ENDINGS TO GERMAN ADJECTIVES**

Adjective	+ –er	English
interessant	interessanter	more interesting
komisch	komischer	funnier, more comical
laut	lauter	louder
reich	reicher	richer
schön	schöner	nicer, prettier

 Essential

Notice that longer words in German still form their comparative meaning by adding –er (interessanter) and do not require a different formation as in English (more interesting).

Adjectives with an umlaut vowel (a, o, u) and adjectives that have only one syllable tend to add an umlaut in the comparative.

▼ **COMPARATIVE FORMS THAT TAKE UMLAUTS**

Adjective	+ –er and Umlaut	English
alt	älter	older
arm	ärmer	poorer
groß	größer	bigger
jung	jünger	younger
kurz	kürzer	shorter
lang	länger	longer

If the adjective ends in –er or –el, you drop the –e when you add the comparative ending.

Adjective	+ –er with a Dropped –e	English
sauer	saurer	sourer
dunkel	dunkler	darker

So groß wie . . .

When you want to show an equality between two things or persons, you can use the phrase *so . . . wie . . .* (as . . . as . . .). In this phrase, the adjective will not require an adjective ending and is not changed to its comparative form. Take a look at some examples.

groß: Hans ist so groß wie sein Bruder.
(Hans is as big as his brother.)

klein: Tina ist so klein wie ihre Schwester.
(Tina is as little as her sister.)

klug: Mein Onkel ist so klug wie mein Schwager.
(My uncle is as smart as my brother-in-law.)

dunkel: Die Dachstube ist so dunkel wie der Keller.
(The attic is as dark as the cellar.)

intelligent: Die Studentin is ebenso intelligent wie der Professor.
(The student is as intelligent as the professor.)

reich: Seine Tante ist ebenso reich wie seine Großmutter.
(His aunt is as rich as his grandmother.)

🚨 Alert

The word *ebenso* is another variation of *so* and can be substituted for the word *so* in these phrases: *Er ist so klein wie Hans. Er ist ebenso klein wie Hans.* (He is as small as Hans.)

Using *als* in a Comparison

When you compare two things and judge one to be of a greater or lesser degree of a certain quality, you use *als* (than) with the comparative adjective. The same will be true if you use a comparative adverb. In these cases, as in the previous examples, there is no need for an adjective ending.

groß: Unser Haus ist größer als euer Haus.
(Our house is bigger than your house.)

langsam: Anna spricht langsamer als Heidi.
(Anna speaks slower than Heidi.)

arm: Sein Vetter ist ärmer als seine Tante.
(His cousin is poorer than his aunt.)

schnell: Mit dem Zug kommen wir schneller nach Hause als mit dem Bus.
(We'll get home faster on the train than on the bus.)

warm: Der Kaffee ist nicht wärmer als der Tee.
(The coffee isn't warmer than the tea.)

intelligent: Andreas ist viel intelligenter als Jens.
(Andreas is much more intelligent than Jens.)

jung: Klaus kann nicht jünger sein als Benno.
(Klaus can't be younger than Benno.)

Just like English, German has a few peculiar forms to worry about. Just as "good" becomes "better" in English, the adjective *gut* changes to *besser* in the German comparative. There are a few others to remember as well:

gut/besser: Er spielt besser als ich.
(He plays better than me.)

bald/eher or *früher: Wir fahren früher.*
(We're leaving [driving] earlier.)

gern/lieber: Hans spielt lieber Schach.
(Hans prefers to play chess.)

hoch/höher: Der Wolkenkratzer ist höher als die Kirche.
(The skyscraper is higher than the church.)

viel/mehr: Sie haben mehr Zeit als wir.
(They have more time than we do.)

Good . . . Better . . . Best

Now that you know the comparative form of adjectives, it's time to learn the superlative degree. The superlative is used to show the person or thing that has the greatest or least degree of a certain quality. In English it is formed by adding *–est* to the adjective or adverb—tall, taller, tallest—or by using the word "most" with longer adjectives: interesting, more interesting, most interesting. German is similar. The German superlative is formed by adding *–st* to an adjective or adverb.

▼ FORMING THE SUPERLATIVE

Adjective	+ –st	English
klein	*kleinst*	smallest
schön	*schönst*	nicest, prettiest
langsam	*langsamst*	slowest

If the adjective ends in *–d, –t, –s, –ss, –ß,* or *–z,* add an *–e* before putting on the superlative ending. Notice also that the short adjectives also take umlauts over the letters *a, o,* or *u,* just as they do in the comparative.

▼ SUPERLATIVE FORMS THAT ADD AN *-E*

Adjective	+ *-est*	English
heiß	*heißest*	hottest
alt	*ältest*	oldest
kurz	*kürzest*	shortest

But the forms listed in the previous table are not complete. A superlative adjective is a modifier and requires an ending. When it is a predicative adjective (standing alone at the end of a phrase) or an adverb, it is preceded by the preposition *am*: *am kleinsten* (the littlest), *am ältesten* (the oldest), *am schönsten* (the nicest or prettiest). Let's look at a few example sentences.

Seine Schwester ist am kleinsten.	His sister is the littlest.
Das weiße Pferd läuft am schnellsten.	The white horse runs the fastest.
Er glaubt, dass sein Urgroßvater am ältesten ist.	He believes that his great-grandfather is the oldest.

There are a few irregular superlatives that you should also be familiar with.

▼ IRREGULAR SUPERLATIVES

Positive	Comparative	Superlative	English
groß	*größer*	*am größten*	biggest
gut	*besser*	*am besten*	best
gern	*lieber*	*am liebsten*	most liked, most preferable
hoch	*höher*	*am höchsten*	highest
nah	*näher*	*am nächsten*	nearest
viel	*mehr*	*am meisten*	most

When the comparative or superlative adjective modifies a noun directly, it requires an adjective ending like any other adjective. Remember that the form *am kleinsten* is used as a predicate adjective. Look at how adjective endings are used in the following examples:

Positive: *Das ist eine gute Idee!*
(That's a good idea.)
Comparative: *Das ist eine bessere Idee!*
(That's a better idea.)
Superlative: *Das ist die beste Idee!*
(That's the best idea.)

Positive: *Es gibt ein dunkles Zimmer im Keller.*
(There's a dark room in the cellar.)
Comparative: *Es gibt ein dunkleres Zimmer im Keller.*
(There's a darker room in the cellar.)
Superlative: *Das dunkelste Zimmer ist im Keller.*
(The darkest room is in the cellar.)

Exercise 17-3

Give the comparative and superlative for each adjective below. For example, when presented with the adjective *klein*, you say, *kleiner, am kleinsten*.

1. *schlecht* _____
2. *sauber* _____
3. *groß* _____
4. *hoch* _____
5. *hübsch* _____
6. *faul* (lazy) _____
7. *klein* _____
8. *laut* _____
9. *interessant* _____
10. *gern* _____

CHAPTER 18

Ifs, Ands, and Buts

Conjunctions (words like "and," "or," and "but") help us put our thoughts together. You can connect sentences in a meaningful way when you know how to use conjunctions properly. You'll also encounter some new prepositions that will come in handy.

Und, oder, aber, and denn

A word that connects two or more clauses is a conjunction. You encountered the conjunctions *und* and *oder* in previous chapters. *Und* (and) lets you combine two or more ideas: the boy **and** the girl. Tom is working in the kitchen, **and** Barbara is working in the garage. *Oder* (or) tells you what options you have: a book **or** a magazine. You can sleep in the attic, **or** you can sleep on the floor. The conjunction *aber* (but) puts two ideas together, but it shows a contrast: It's sunny, **but** a storm is brewing. She was very happy, **but** tears streamed down her face.

Some commonly used English conjunctions include "and," "but," "or," "because," "that," "if," and "as if." Look how they combine sentences:

She gets sick. I call the doctor.
She gets sick, and I call the doctor.

She gives him a dollar. He says nothing.
She gives him a dollar, but he says nothing.

I sleep till ten. I go to bed very late.

I sleep till ten because I go to bed very late.

German conjunctions function in the same way, and many of them require no special rules for using them. *Und* (and), *aber* (but), *oder* (or), and *denn* (because) are four such conjunctions, and they put sentences together just like their English counterparts.

Sie ist krank. Ich rufe den Arzt an.

Sie ist krank und ich rufe den Arzt an.

She is sick, and I call the doctor.

Sie gibt ihm zwei Dollar. Er sagt nichts.

Sie gibt ihm zwei Dollar, aber er sagt nichts.

She gives him two dollars, but he says nothing.

Ich schlafe bis zehn. Ich gehe spät ins Bett.

Ich schlafe bis zehn, denn ich gehe spät ins Bett.

I sleep until ten because I go to bed late.

Kannst du hier bleiben? Musst du schon nach Hause gehen?

Kannst du hier bleiben, oder musst du schon nach Hause gehen?

Can you stay here or do you have to go home already?

You'll notice that each of these conjunctions combines two complete sentences. Each one has a subject and a verb, and, just like other sentences with normal word order, the subject comes before the verb in each. However, there are other conjunctions that require a change in the order of the sentence.

Alert

Careful! Don't confuse the conjunction *denn* (because) with the genitive preposition *wegen* (because of, on account of). They have similar meanings, but confusing them will certainly confuse your conversation partner! Be sure you can recognize the subtle differences between the two.

Conjunctions That Affect Word Order

German has other conjunctions that are important to know and are frequently used. Four of these are *dass* (that), *weil* (because), *wenn* (whenever or if), and *als* (when). They act like the other German conjunctions and combine sentences and clauses. But these four are special; when they're used in a sentence, the conjugated verb has to be placed at the very end of the clause in which the conjunction occurs.

Ich wusste nicht, dass du Österreicher bist.
I didn't know that you are an Austrian.

Sie ist traurig, weil ihr Vater gestorben ist.
She is sad because her father died.

Wenn ich in Berlin bin, besuche ich meinen Onkel.
Whenever I'm in Berlin, I visit my uncle.

Als er in der Stadt war, ging er ins Theater.
When he was in the city, he went to the theater.

Both *denn* and *weil* mean "because." *Denn* follows the rules of normal word order. *Weil* requires the verb at the end of the clause:

Sie ist traurig, denn ihr Vater ist gestorben.
She is sad because her father died.

Sie ist traurig, weil ihr Vater gestorben ist.
She is sad because her father died.

When you wish to convey the meaning of "whenever," use *wenn*. The conjunction *als* means "when" in the past tense:

Wenn ich in Berlin bin, besuche ich meine Tante.
Whenever I'm in Berlin, I visit my aunt.

Als ich in Berlin war, besuchte ich meine Tante.
When I was in Berlin, I visited my aunt.

Be aware that *wenn* can be used in all tenses, but the meaning must be "whenever."

Interrogatives Used as Conjunctions

Interrogative words ask questions: who? what? why? where? when? how? The German interrogatives that you've encountered so far are: *wer* (who), *wen* (whom), *wem* (whom), *wessen* (whose), *was* (what), *was für* (what kind of), *warum* (why), *wann* (when), *wie* (how), *wo* (where), and *welcher* (which).

In addition to asking questions, the interrogatives can be used to combine two sentences, often acting as the response to a question: "Who took the newspaper?" "I don't know who took the newspaper." Let's look at how this works in English.

Who's at the door?	I don't know who's at the door.
Where is her father?	No one knows where her father is.
When did he die?	The woman didn't say when he died.
Whose wallet did Tom find?	It's not clear whose wallet Tom found.

The German interrogatives function in the same way. The only difference is that when they're used in an indirect response, the conjugated verb becomes the last element in the sentence: *Wer ist das? Ich weiß nicht, wer das ist.* Take a look at some examples in German.

Wer ist im Garten?	*Ich weiß nicht, wer im Garten ist.*
	I don't know who's in the garden.
Wen besucht Hans?	*Wir wissen nicht, wen Hans besucht.*
	We don't know whom Hans is visiting.
Mit wem spricht sie?	*Wir wissen nicht, mit wem sie spricht.*
	We don't know whom she's talking with.
Wessen Hut hast du gefunden?	*Ich weiß nicht, wessen Hut ich gefunden habe.*
	I don't know whose hat I found.
Was bedeutet das?	*Er sagte nicht, was das bedeutet.*
	He didn't say what that meant.
Was für ein Student ist er?	*Sie weiß nicht, was für ein Student er ist.*
	She doesn't know what kind of student he is.
Warum sind sie so arm?	*Niemand weiß, warum sie so arm sind.*
	No one knows why they're so poor.
Wann kommt der Zug?	*Ich weiß nicht, wann der Zug kommt.*
	I don't know when the train comes.
Wie alt ist Sabine?	*Wir wissen nicht, wie alt Sabine ist.*
	We don't know how old Sabine is.
Wo ist Ludwig?	*Niemand weiß, wo Ludwig ist.*
	No one knows where Ludwig is.
Welchen Roman hat er gelesen?	*Es ist mir egal, welchen Roman er gelesen hat*
	I don't care what novel he read.

You probably noticed that *wann* is the third German word you've learned that can mean "when." Just remember that *wann* is used to ask questions, *wenn* is used for the meaning "whenever," and *als* means "when" in the past tense.

Exercise 18-1

Complete the sentence *Ich weiß nicht, . . .* with the following questions. For example, when presented with the question *Wo ist Ludwig?*, you say, *Ich weiß nicht, wo Ludwig ist.* (I don't know where Ludwig is.)

1. *Wer hat das Fenster gebrochen?* (Who broke the window?)

    _____

2. *Wen will Mutter besuchen?* (Whom does Mother want to visit?)

    _____

3. *Wann fliegt das Flugzeug?* (When does the plane leave?)

    _____

4. *Welches Hemd möchte Jens haben?* (Which shirt would Jens like
    to have?)

    _____

5. *Was für einen Wagen hat Vater gekauft?* (What kind of car did
    Father buy?)

    _____

More Than Just *der*, *die*, and *das*

You recognize *der*, *die*, and *das* as definitive articles. But these words also have another use in German. They are also relative pronouns.

A relative pronoun refers to someone or something already mentioned in a sentence. English speakers use who, that, and which.

Where's the man who needs a doctor?
They finally found the car that was stolen.
The book that he chose for his report is too short.

German forms the same kind of constructions, which are called relative clauses, but uses the definite articles in place of the words who, that, and which. And, of course, gender plays a key role. If the person or thing you're talking about is masculine, you have to use *der* as the relative pronoun. If it's feminine or plural, use *die*. If it's neuter, use *das*. Then, the conjugated verb has to stand at the end of the clause.

Take a look at some examples.

Ich kenne den Mann, der an der Ecke steht.
I know the man who's standing on the corner.

Seine Freundin, die aus Schweden kommt, will Lehrerin werden.
His girlfriend, who comes from Sweden, wants to become a teacher.

Ich sehe die Kinder, die ins Kino gehen.
I see the children who are going to the movies.

Sie kaufen ein Haus, das sehr alt ist.
They are buying a house that is very old.

This usage of *der, die*, and *das* as relative pronouns is easy to identify. Look for two things: (1) The gender of the article is the same as the noun to which it refers, and (2) the conjugated verb in the clause is at the end of the sentence. *Er findet einen Hund,* (1) <u>*der*</u> *alt und krank* (2) <u>*ist.*</u> (He finds a dog that is old and sick.) Remember to translate this usage of *der, die*, and *das* as who, that, and which.

Of course, if the relative pronoun is used as a subject, it will be in the nominative case as shown in the previous examples. But relative pronouns can appear in the other cases—dative, accusative, or genitive—as well. Although the relative pronouns are different from definite articles, they still change with the functions of the cases just like definite articles.

Accusative Direct Object: *Wo ist der Student, den Sabine liebt?*
Where is the student that Sabine loves?

Dative Preposition: *Wo ist der Diplomat, mit dem Karl gesprochen hat?*
Where is the diplomat that Karl spoke with?

A New Kind of Preposition

You've discovered how German prepositions are categorized according to the case they're used with: dative prepositions, accusative prepositions, and genitive prepositions. There's one more category, and it includes the prepositions that can be used either in the dative case or in the accusative case.

How can that happen? It's really not so tricky. In English, sometimes there are pairs of prepositions that are similar but are used in a specific way. One of those pairs is "in/into." You can't say, "I'll wait for you *into* the kitchen." The preposition "into" is used to show motion toward some place. "I ran into the kitchen." "She fell into a hole." It is the preposition "in" that shows location and is used to say something like, "I'll wait for you *in* the kitchen."

This same kind of distinction is what the dative-accusative prepositions identify in German. But instead of having pairs of prepositions (in/into, on/onto), German uses two different case endings to make the differentiation.

▼ PREPOSITIONS THAT CAN TAKE DATIVE OR ACCUSATIVE

German	English	German	English
an	at	*über*	over
auf	on	*unter*	under
hinter	behind	*vor*	in front of
in	in	*zwischen*	between
neben	next to		

The dative case is used if you're talking about location, and the accusative case is used when you are talking about motion. Take the preposition *in* as an example. When standing alone, *in* simply means "in" and is used very much like the same English word. But the German word *in* has two meanings: "in" and "into." When it means "in," it is followed by the dative case. When it means "into," it is followed by the accusative case.

So if you say, "I'm in school today," you use the dative case: *in der Schule*. But if you say, "I'm hurrying into the school," you use the accusative case: *in die Schule*. With masculine nouns, you have *im Schrank* (in the closet) and *in den Schrank* (into the closet). *Im* is the contraction of *in dem*.

Neuter nouns follow the same pattern: *im Kino* (in the movie house, at the movies) and *ins Kino* (into the movie house, to the movies). *Ins* is the contraction of *in das*.

▼ PREPOSITIONS AND CONTRACTIONS

Prepositional Phrase	Contraction	Prepositional Phrase	Contraction
an das	*ans*	*in dem*	*im*
an dem	*am*	*von dem*	*vom*
auf das	*aufs*	*zu dem*	*zum*
in das	*ins*	*zu der*	*zur*

The other prepositions function the same way as *in*. Look at these pairs of sentences that use prepositions with both the dative case (to indicate location) and the accusative case (to indicate motion).

Location: *Sie steht am Fenster.* (She is standing at the window.)
Motion: *Sie geht ans Fenster.* (She goes to the window.)

Location: *Die Vase steht auf dem Tisch.* (The vase is on the table.)
Motion: *Ich stelle die Vase auf den Tisch.* (I place the vase on the table.)

Location: *Ich stand hinter der Tür.* (I stood behind the door.)
Motion: *Ich stellte mich hinter die Tür.* (I placed myself behind the door.)

Location: *Wir sind im Wohnzimmer.* (We're in the living room.)
Motion: *Wir kommen ins Wohnzimmer.* (We come into the living room.)

Location: *Ich stehe neben dem Mann.* (I stand next to the man.)
Motion: *Ich setze mich neben den Mann.* (I sit down next to the man.)

Location: *Ein Bild hängt über dem Tisch.* (A picture is hanging over the table.)
Motion: *Er hängt ein Bild über den Tisch.* (He hangs a picture over the table.)

Location: *Der Hund schläft unter dem Tisch.* (The dog is sleeping under the table.)
Motion: *Der Hund läuft unter den Tisch.* (The dog runs under the table.)

Location: *Ich stand vor einem Spiegel.* (I stood in front of a mirror.)
Motion: *Ich gehe vor einen Spiegel.* (I walk in front of a mirror.)

Location: *Sie steht zwischen ihren Eltern.* (She stands between her parents.)

Motion: *Sie stellt sich zwischen ihre Eltern.* (She places herself between her parents.)

Exercise 18-2

Complete the sentences below with the correct word or phrase from the two provided in parentheses. For example, when presented with the phrases *Er stand Tür (vor die, vor der)*, you say, *Er stand vor der Tür.* (He stood in front of the door.) In this sentence *vor* is describing location, which is shown by the dative case.

1. *Wir sehen die Kinder _____ Garten.* (*in dem, in den*)
2. *Die Zeitungen waren _____ Heft.* (*neben dem, neben das*)
3. *Vater ging langsam _____ Tür.* (*an der, an die*)
4. *Die Kinder laufen _____ Haus.* (*hinter dem, hinter das*)
5. *Mein Vetter sitzt _____ Frau.* (*neben seiner, neben seine*)
6. *Die Jungen spielen _____ Park.* (*im, in den*)
7. *Er stellt die Vase _____ Klavier.* (*auf dem, auf das*)
8. *Was hängt _____ Tisch?* (*über dem, über den*)
9. *Sie läuft _____ Küche.* (*in der, in die*)
10. *Wer steht _____ Ecke?* (*an der, an die*)

CHAPTER 19

Talking about the Subjunctive

The subjunctive mood is used less often in English, but it is still thriving in the German language. It's useful for situations such as speculation or indirect discourse, when you want to tell someone what someone else has said: He said I should learn German. Verbs in the subjunctive use forms and endings that you already know, so putting it all together will be a breeze.

The Ones That Cling to Life

Many English speakers still use the subjunctive to express a proposal or a suggestion, and it is still used in certain legal phrases. The following examples demonstrate some of the different usages that remain in English.

Proposal: The proposal stated he pay for all construction costs. (not "he pays")

Recommendation: The doctor recommended she rest from her chores. (not "she rests")

Suggestion: We suggested she be on time. (not "she is")

Command: The king commanded the army stand fast. (not "the army stands")

Legal phrase: The judge ruled the defendant be held over until tomorrow. (not "the defendant is")

Wishes

When expressing a wish, there is still often a feeling for the subjunctive in English. Many people avoid it, but it's not a form that sounds weird or out of place—perhaps just a little fancy: "I wish Mother were here right now." The conjugation of "to be" with the subject "Mother" should be "is" or "was," but in a wish the verb "to be" becomes exclusively "were." Of course, you'll hear just as frequently: "I wish Mother was here right now."

If . . .

Sentences that begin with "if" are expressing a condition: "If this were the case, that would happen." Some sentences consist of just one phrase: "If only John were here." "If only I had eaten only one piece of cake!"

But frequently there are two clauses united by "if": "If it were to storm [that's the condition], we would have to stay in our tents." "If your mother could hear you now [the condition], you'd be sorry."

Very often the word "would" plays a role in these sentences. It's another holdout from the old days of the subjunctive voice:

Condition: Mother is here
Conditional sentence: If Mother were here, you would act differently.

Condition: The rain stops
Conditional sentence: If the rain stopped, we would run to the lake for a swim.

Condition: John has helped
Conditional sentence: If John had helped, we would have been done an hour ago.

Condition: He has met Mary
Conditional sentence: If he had met Mary, he would have fallen in love.

Condition: She has won the lottery
Conditional sentence: If she had won the lottery, she would have traveled around the world.

Did you notice the tense changes in the above examples? The same sentence can be expressed in two ways. One tells what would happen now, if only the conditions were right: "If the rain stopped, we would go for a swim." The other tells what would have happened in the past: "If the rain had stopped, we would have gone for a swim."

Having some idea of what traces of the English subjunctive remain makes it easier to grasp the German subjunctive. It's not as hard as it might seem. German is our sister language. There are always similarities to guide you.

He Said . . . She Said . . .

One widely used form of German subjunctive is with indirect discourse. What's that? Direct discourse is a direct quote: Bill said, "Tom is dancing with my girl." Indirect discourse is a report of what was said: Bill said that Tom is dancing with his girl.

This subjunctive conjugational form is called Subjunctive I. It is formed using the verb stem derived from the infinitive of the verb. Some rather familiar endings are then attached to the stem. The Subjunctive I is used less often than the Subjunctive II mood. Germans often avoid using Subjunctive I by using either the indicative or the Subjunctive II, but it is read and heard frequently in news reporting.

▼ CONJUGATIONAL ENDINGS—SUBJUNCTIVE I

Person	Ending to Add to Verb Stem	Example
First (sing.)	–e	*ich habe*
Second (sing.)	–est	*du habest*
Third (sing.)	–e	*er/sie/es habe*
First (pl.)	–en	*wir haben*
Second (pl.)	–et	*ihr habet*
Second (formal)	–en	*Sie haben*
Third (pl.)	–en	*sie haben*

You'll notice that the subjunctive of the verb *haben* is slightly different than the form you already know (which is called the indicative). In the subjunctive, all irregularities of the present tense are ignored: *du habest* not *du hast*, *er sehe* not *er sieht*, *du wollest* not *du willst*, *sie schlafe* not *sie schläft*. Let's look at the conjugations of a few other verbs you know well.

▼ SUBJUNCTIVE I CONJUGATIONS

Pronoun	gehen	wollen	trinken
ich	gehe	wolle	trinke
du	gehest	wollest	trinkest
er/sie/es	gehe	wolle	trinke
wir	gehen	wollen	trinken
ihr	gehet	wollet	trinket
Sie	gehen	wollen	trinken
sie (pl.)	gehen	wollen	trinken

The verb *sein* is special. With the pronouns *ich, er, sie,* and *es,* the verb has no ending: *sei.*

▼ SUBJUNCTIVE I CONJUGATION OF *SEIN*

Pronoun	Conjugation	Pronoun	Conjugation
ich	sei	wir	seien
du	seiest	ihr	seiet
er/sie/es	sei	Sie	seien
		sie (pl.)	seien

As previously noted, because English doesn't have a Subjunctive I conjugation, you can't directly translate what the conjugations mean. They have a specific function, and that is to report what someone else said, called indirect discourse.

Der Verdächtigte sagte, dass er den Wagen nicht gestohlen habe.
The suspect said he didn't steal the car.

Die Studenten erzählten uns, dass sie nie nach Italien gereist seien.
The students told us they have never been to Italy.

Der Politiker verspricht, das er alles besser mache.
The politician promises to do everything better.

The Past Tense of the Subjunctive Mood

There is another subjunctive conjugation, which we'll call Subjunctive II. It is formed from the past tense stem of the verb (both regular and irregular!). The endings that are used to form the conjugations are the same as for the Subjunctive I. In the case of regular verbs, the Subjunctive II conjugation is identical to the regular past tense. Let's look first at the conjugations of a regular verb.

▼ **SUBJUNCTIVE II CONJUGATIONS OF REGULAR VERBS**

Pronoun	Conjugation	Pronoun	Conjugation
ich	fragte	wir	fragten
du	fragtest	ihr	fragtet
er/sie/es	fragte	Sie	fragten
		sie (pl.)	fragten

Conjugating irregular verbs (verbs that have a stem change) in the Subjunctive II looks a lot like the past tense of these verbs. But watch out for the umlaut! All irregular verbs that have an umlaut vowel, plus all the modal auxiliaries except for *wollen* and *sollen*, add an umlaut in this conjugation. Regular verbs do not add an umlaut.

▼ **SUBJUNCTIVE II CONJUGATIONS OF IRREGULAR VERBS**

Pronoun	*haben*	*sein*	*gehen*	*wollen*
ich	hätte	wäre	ginge	wollte
du	hättest	wärest	gingest	wolltest
er/sie/es	hätte	wäre	ginge	wollte
wir	hätten	wären	gingen	wollten
ihr	hättet	wäret	ginget	wolltet
Sie	hätten	wären	gingen	wollten
sie (pl.)	hätten	wären	gingen	wollten

Exercise 19-1

Rewrite each infinitive in the Subjunctive I and the Subjunctive II for the pronoun *er*. For example, if presented with the infinitive *haben*, you say *(er) habe hätte*.

1. *sein*   _____   _____
2. *ansehen*   _____   _____
3. *warten*   _____   _____
4. *bekommen*   _____   _____
5. *wissen*   _____   _____
6. *müssen*   _____   _____
7. *kaufen*   _____   _____
8. *trinken*   _____   _____
9. *essen*   _____   _____
10. *lernen*   _____   _____

Use these conjugations when you are conveying the information provided by what someone said, reported, or wrote. When you tell someone else what you heard another party say, what that party said is an indirect quote. The verb in the quote has to be in the subjunctive.

Look at direct discourse first: *Andreas sagte, "Der Lehrer hat keine Zeit."* (Andreas said, "The teacher has no time.") When this is changed to indirect discourse, the result is: *Andreas sagte, dass der Lehrer keine Zeit habe.* (Andreas said that the teacher has no time.) Or you can use the Subjunctive II conjugation: *Andreas sagte, dass der Lehrer keine Zeit hätte.* (Andreas said that the teacher had no time.) The use of the Subjunctive II conjugation sounds less formal.

When the regular present tense conjugation is the same as the Subjunctive I conjugation, you should use the Subjunctive II form to make it obvious that you're speaking about indirect discourse. If the original quotation is in the Subjunctive II, then the indirect quote also uses the Subjunctive II.

These sentences changed from direct to indirect discourse. The subjunctive can be used in either form, so both are given in the examples:

Direct discourse: *Maria wird Lehrerin.*

(Maria is becoming a teacher.)
Indirect discourse: *Er sagte, dass Maria Lehrerin werde (würde).*
(He said that Maria is becoming a teacher.)

Direct discourse: *Er besucht seinen Onkel.*
(He visits his uncle.)
Indirect discourse: *Er sagte, dass er seinen Onkel besuche (besuchte).*
(He said that he was visiting his uncle.)

Direct discourse: *Seine Eltern kommen bald nach Hause.*
(His parents are coming home soon.)
Indirect discourse: *Ich sagte, dass seine Eltern bald nach Hause kämen.*
(I said that his parents were coming home soon.)

If the sentence in direct discourse is in one of the past tenses, use the present perfect tense in indirect discourse with the auxiliary verb (*haben, sein*) conjugated in the subjunctive.

Direct discourse: *Maria hat ihn gesehen.*
(Maria had seen him.)
Indirect discourse: *Er schrieb, dass Maria ihn gesehen habe (hätte).*
(He wrote that Maria had seen him.)

Direct discourse: *Karl hat das Geld gefunden.*
(Karl has found the money.)
Indirect discourse: *Er schrieb, dass Karl das Geld gefunden habe (hätte).*
(He wrote that Karl has found the money.)

Direct discourse: *Sie sind nach Berlin gefahren.*
(They drove to Berlin.)
Indirect discourse: *Er schrieb, dass sie nach Berlin gefahren seien (wären).*
(He wrote that they drove to Berlin.)

Direct discourse: *Tina ist Lehrerin geworden.*

(Tina became a teacher.)

Indirect discourse: *Er schrieb, dass Tina Lehrerin geworden sei (wäre).*

(He wrote that Tina became a teacher.)

Exercise 19-2

Restate the following sentences as indirect discourse (using either the Subjunctive I or II) with the phrase *Mutter sagte, dass. . . .* For example, when presented with the sentence *Frau Meier ist wieder krank*, you write, *Mutter sagte, dass Frau Meier wieder krank sei (wäre).* (Mother said that Ms. Meier is sick again.)

1. *Unser alter Freund wird zu Besuch kommen.* (Our old friend will come for a visit.)

   _____

2. *Sie hat ihre neue Brille verloren.* (She has lost her new glasses.)

   _____

3. *Jens soll seine Hausaufgaben machen.* (Jens should do his homework.)

   _____

4. *Es wird bald ein Gewitter geben.* (There's going to be a thunderstorm soon.)

   _____

5. *Vater kann nicht mehr arbeiten.* (Father cannot work anymore.)

   _____

-

One More Use for *wenn*!

Previously you learned to differentiate among the three words that can mean "when" in German: *wann*, *als*, and *wenn*. Well, there's one more use for the conjunction *wenn*: It's used with a Subjunctive II conjugation and means "if."

Just like the English "if" phrase, the German *wenn* phrase sets a condition for some further action. "If it snowed [the condition], we would go sledding." The German sentence is constructed in exactly the same way, but the conjugated verb in the *wenn* phrase must stand at the end of the phrase. And, of course, the verbs in both clauses are conjugated in Subjunctive II: *Wenn er nicht krank wäre, würde er mit den Kindern spielen.* (If he weren't sick, he would play with the children.) Did you notice the verb *würde*? It's used just like the English word "would" and is followed by an infinitive.

Here are more examples to consider.

Wenn ich reich wäre, würde ich einen neuen Wagen kaufen.
If I were rich, I would buy a new car.

Wenn er in Berlin wohnte, würde er oft ins Theater gehen.
If he lived in Berlin, he would go to the theater often.

Wir würden Schach spielen, wenn wir Zeit hätten.
We would play chess if we had time.

Ich würde das nicht tun, wenn ich du wäre.
I would not do that if I were you.

Wenn ich Geld gehabt hätte, hätte ich ein großes Haus gekauft.
If I had had money, I would have bought a big house.

Wenn es nicht so dunkel gewesen wäre, hätten wir die Straße gefunden.
If it hadn't been so dark, we would have found the street.

Wenn sie nicht krank geworden wäre, hätte sie mir geholfen.
If she hadn't become sick, she would have helped me.

Wenn ich Deutsch gekonnt hätte, hätte ich mit ihm gesprochen.
If I had known German, I would have spoken with him.

Look at the last four sentences. When the verb structure is composed of an auxiliary and participle, you can avoid using *würde* in the phrase.

Als ob

There is one more instance when the Subjunctive II conjugation is needed. The conjunction *als ob* (as if) requires the verb in the phrase that follows to be in Subjunctive II and that the verb be placed at the end of the sentence. Sometimes this conjunction appears as *als wenn* instead of *als ob*.

Andreas sieht aus, als ob er krank geworden wäre.
Andreas looks like (as if) he has become ill.

Mutter tat, als ob sie mich nicht verstanden hätte.
Mother acted like she hadn't understood me.

Er sah aus, als ob er verrückt wäre.
He looked like he was crazy.

Sabine hat so getan, als ob sie sehr reich wäre.
Sabine acted as if she were very rich.

Answer Key

Chapter 2

Exercise 2-1

1. *Wie geht es Ihnen, Professor Braun?*
2. *Wie geht's, Angelika?*
3. *Wie geht's, Hans?*
4. *Wie geht es Ihnen, Frau Keller?*
5. *Wie geht es Ihnen, Herr Doktor?*

Exercise 2-2

1. *Wie heißt die Frau? Die Frau heißt Maria Schmidt.*
2. *Wie heißt der Student? Der Student heißt Karl.*
3. *Wie heißt die Studentin? Die Studentin heißt Anna.*
4. *Wie heißt der Ausländer? Der Ausländer heißt Tom Smith.*

Chapter 3

Exercise 3-1

1. *der Mantel*
2. *die Ausstellung*
3. *das Gelächter*
4. *die Klasse*

5. *der Brunnen*
6. *die Sprache*
7. *das Männchen*
8. *die Prüfung*
9. *die Wissenschaft*
10. *das Essen*

Exercise 3-2
1. *ein Lehrer*
2. *eine Schauspielerin*
3. *eine Tasse*
4. *ein Pilot*
5. *ein Mädchen*
6. *der Mantel*
7. *die Lehrerin*
8. *das Kind*
9. *der Bruder*
10. *der Richter*

Chapter 4

Exercise 4-1
1. *die Äpfel*
2. *die Blumen*
3. *die Bücher*
4. *die Gärten*
5. *die Stunden*

Exercise 4-2
1. *Sie ist in der Schule.*
2. *Sind sie hier?*
3. *Er ist in Deutschland.*
4. *Wir sind Amerikaner.*
5. *Wo ist sie?*

Exercise 4-3

1. *Die neue Vase ist gelb.*
2. *Der alte BMW ist braun.*
3. *Die Rose ist rot.*
4. *Der neue Mantel ist blau.*
5. *Das Haus ist grau.*

Chapter 5

Exercise 5-1

1. *Ich bin in Berlin.* (I am in Berlin.)
2. *Er ist in Hamburg.* (He is in Hamburg.)
3. *Wir sind in Deutschland.* (We are in Germany.)
4. *Du bist in Amerika.* (You are in America.)
5. *Karl ist in Frankfurt.* (Karl is in Frankfurt.)

Exercise 5-2

1. *ist*
2. *sind*
3. *seid*
4. *bist*
5. *sind*
6. *ist*
7. *bin*
8. *ist*
9. *ist*
10. *sind*

Exercise 5-3

1. *geht*
2. *fährt*
3. *kaufe*
4. *trinkt*
5. *kommt*

Chapter 6

Exercise 6-1
1. *Morgen geht er ins Kino.*
2. *Morgen fliegen sie nach Hause.*
3. *Morgen gehe ich ins Museum.*
4. *Morgen kommt Ludwig nicht ins Restaurant.*
5. *Morgen fährst du in die Stadt.*

Exercise 6-2
1. *Das Kind spricht kein Deutsch.*
2. *Du schläfst im Wohnzimmer.*
3. *Siehst du die Alpen?*
4. *Peter hilft Frau Meier.*
5. *Vater trifft meine Freundin.*

Exercise 6-3
1. *fahren*	*ich fahre*	*er fährt*
2. *mitkommen*	*ich komme mit*	*er kommt mit*
3. *bekommen*	*ich bekomme*	*er bekommt*
4. *lesen*	*ich lese*	*er liest*
5. *verstehen*	*ich verstehe*	*er versteht*
6. *sprechen*	*ich spreche*	*er spricht*
7. *beibringen*	*ich bringe bei*	*er bringt bei*
8. *fallen*	*ich falle*	*er fällt*
9. *aufhören*	*ich höre auf*	*er hört auf*
10. *erwarten*	*ich erwarte*	*er erwartet*

Chapter 7

Exercise 7-1
1. *Sie haben sie.*
2. *Sie haben sie.*
3. *Haben Sie sie?*
4. *Sehen Sie es?*
5. *Hans und Andreas sehen ihn nicht.*

Exercise 7-2
1. *Die Jungen kommen ohne Peter. Die Jungen kommen ohne meine Schwester.*
2. *Wir fahren mit dem Wagen um das Schloss. Wir fahren mit dem Wagen um die Kirche.*
3. *Ich gehe durch das Haus. Ich gehe durch den Bahnhof.*
4. *Sie hat ein Buch für Frau Schneider. Sie hat ein Buch für das Mädchen.*
5. *Bist du gegen mich? Bist du gegen uns?*

Chapter 8

Exercise 8-1
1. *Ich gebe dem Lehrer mein Heft.*
2. *Er sendet der Dame einen Brief.*
3. *Frau Schmidt bringt dem Schüler ein Glas Wasser.*
4. *Wir geben dem Kellner das Geld.*
5. *Was gibst du der Studentin?*

Chapter 9

Exercise 9-1
1. *Was kaufe ich?*
2. *Wohin gehen wir morgen?*
3. *Was sucht der Student?*

4. *Wann fliegen sie nach New York?*
5. *Was findet Sabine?*

Exercise 9-2

1. *Wem glaubt er nicht?*
2. *Mit wem kommt Sabine?*
3. *Wem folgen die Kinder?*
4. *Bei wem wohnt Herr Braun?*
5. *Nach wem fragt der Professor?*
6. *Mit wem tanzt Martin?*
7. *Von wem ist der Brief?*
8. *Wem hilft Stefan nicht?*
9. *Wem gefällt das Buch nicht?*
10. *Wem gibt Peter das Geld?*

Chapter 10

Exercise 10-1

1. *Wie viel kostet das Brötchen? Das Brötchen kostet zwei Euro und zehn Cent.*
2. *Wie viel kostet die Lampe? Die Lampe kostet sieben Euro und zehn Cent.*
3. *Wie viel kosten der Teller und die Tasse? Der Teller und die Tasse kosten zehn Euro.*
4. *Wie viel kostet das Gemüse? Das Gemüse kostet vier Euro und zehn Cent.*
5. *Wie viel kostet die Milch? Die Milch kostet drei Euro und fünf Cent.*

Chapter 11

Exercise 11-1

1. *Wann kommt Tante Luise? Sie kommt übermorgen.*
2. *Wann kommt der Professor? Er kommt heute Nachtmittag.*
3. *Wann kommt Frau Keller? Sie kommt heute Abend.*
4. *Wann kommt Martin? Er kommt morgen früh.*
5. *Wann kommt Herr Schäfer? Er kommt heute Morgen.*
6. *Wann kommen die Kinder? Sie kommen morgen Abend.*

Exercise 11-2

1. *Um wie viel Uhr ist der Film? Der Film ist um fünfzehn Uhr.*
2. *Um wie viel Uhr ist die Prüfung? Die Prüfung ist um halb elf.*
3. *Um wie viel Uhr ist das Fußballspiel? Das Fußballspiel ist um sechzehn Uhr fünfundvierzig.*
4. *Um wie viel Uhr ist das Konzert? Das Konzert ist um zwanzig Uhr fünfzehn.*
5. *Um wie viel Uhr ist die Geburtstagsparty? Die Geburtstagsparty ist um dreizehn Uhr.*

Exercise 11-3

1. *Wann ist das Konzert? Das Konzert ist am Sonntag.*
2. *Wann ist der Film? Der Film ist am Dienstag.*
3. *Wann ist die Oper? Die Oper ist am Mittwoch.*
4. *Wann ist das Schauspiel? Das Schauspiel ist am Donnerstag.*
5. *Wann ist das Examen? Das Examen ist am Freitag.*

Exercise 11-4

1. *Frau Keller ist im Jahre 1961 geboren.*
2. *Das Baby ist im Jahre 2008 geboren.*
3. *Meine Schwester ist im Jahre 1989 geboren.*
4. *Meine Großmutter ist im Jahre 1939 geboren.*
5. *Herr Schmidt ist im Jahre 1978 geboren.*

Chapter 12

Exercise 12-1

1. *sagen* (say)	*ich sagte*	*sie (s.) sagte*	*sie*	*(pl.)sagten*
2. *kaufen* (buy)	*du kauftest*	*es kaufte*	*wir*	*kauften*
3. *stellen* (put)	*ich stellte*	*ihr stelltet*	*Sie*	*stellten*
4. *reisen* (travel)	*du reistest*	*er reiste*	*wir*	*reisten*
5. *baden* (bathe)	*er badete*	*ihr badetet*	*Sie*	*badeten*

Exercise 12-2

1. *Meine Tante wohnte in den Vereinigten Staaten.*
2. *Ich liebte Brot mit Käse.*
3. *Wohin flogt ihr?*
4. *Ihr spieltet oft Fußball.*
5. *Ich hörte keine Musik.*
6. *Sie ging ins Kino.*
7. *Sprachst du mit Thomas?*
8. *Er sah Frau Schmidt im Büro.*
9. *Die Kinder antworteten auf Französisch.*
10. *Wir sangen auf Deutsch.*

Chapter 13

Exercise 13-1

1. *Die Männer werden Fußball spielen.* (The men will play soccer.)
2. *Er wird in Bayern wohnen.* (He will live in Bavaria.)
3. *Meine Freunde werden in den Alpen sein.* (My friends will be in the Alps.)
4. *Ich werde oft an Heinrich denken.* (I will think often of Heinrich.)
5. *Was werden Sie brauchen?* (What will you need?)
6. *Sabine wird im Kaufhaus arbeiten.* (Sabine will work in the department store.)
7. *Ich werde nur Milch kaufen.* (I will only buy milk.)
8. *Was wirst du machen?* (What will you do?)

9. *Er wird etwas sagen.* (He will say something.)
10. *Wir werden nur Deutsch sprechen.* (We will speak only German.)

Exercise 13-2

1. *Die Kinder lernen Deutsch.*
2. *Ich spreche mit ihm.*
3. *Helga denkt oft an uns.*
4. *Wohnst du in Bremen?*
5. *Erik läuft nach Hause.*

Exercise 13-3

1. *machen*	*mache!*	*macht!*	*machen Sie!*
2. *trinken*	*trinke!*	*trinkt!*	*trinken Sie!*
3. *lesen*	*lies!*	*lest!*	*lesen Sie!*
4. *ansehen*	*sieh an!*	*seht an!*	*sehen Sie an!*
5. *versprechen*	*versprich!*	*versprecht!*	*versprechen Sie!*
6. *warten*	*warte!*	*wartet!*	*warten Sie!*
7. *besuchen*	*besuche!*	*besucht!*	*besuchen Sie!*
8. *mitkommen*	*komme mit!*	*kommt mit!*	*kommen Sie mit!*
9. *schreiben*	*schreibe!*	*schreibt!*	*schreiben Sie!*
10. *glauben*	*glaube!*	*glaubt!*	*glauben Sie!*

Chapter 14

Exercise 14-1

1. *kaufen*	*gekauft*	6. *setzen*	*gesetzt*
2. *stören*	*gestört*	7. *reden*	*geredet*
3. *lehren*	*gelehrt*	8. *baden*	*gebadet*
4. *bauen*	*gebaut*	9. *lachen*	*gelacht*
5. *stellen*	*gestellt*	10. *weinen*	*geweint*

Exercise 14-2

1. *ich habe gefragt* (I have asked)
2. *sie sind gereist* (they have traveled)
3. *du hast gesehen* (you have seen)
4. *wir haben gefunden* (we have found)
5. *ihr seid gewesen* (you all have been)
6. *ich bin geblieben* (I have remained)
7. *wir haben gewusst* (we have known)
8. *du hast gestört* (you have disturbed)
9. *er hat gegessen* (he has eaten)
10. *sie* (pl.) *sind gekommen* (they have come)
11. *du hast gestellt* (you have placed)
12. *Sie sind gegangen* (you have gone)
13. *ich bin gelaufen* (I have run)
14. *er ist gestorben* (he has died)
15. *wir haben genommen* (we have taken)

Exercise 14-3

1. *Hans und Maria waren in den Garten gelaufen.* (Hans and Maria had run in the garden.)
2. *Ich hatte einen Brief von Helga bekommen.* (I had received a letter from Helga.)
3. *Wer hatte den Wagen repariert?* (Who had repaired the car?)
4. *Er hatte mich gefragt.* (He had asked me.)
5. *Ich hatte ein Glas Wasser getrunken.* (I had drunk a glass of water.)
6. *Wer hatte die Frau gekannt?* (Who had known the woman?)
7. *Wir waren nach Berlin gereist.* (We had traveled to Berlin.)
8. *Hattest du das Buch gelesen?* (Had you read the book?)
9. *Er hatte einen Hut getragen.* (He had worn a hat.)
10. *Ich war zu Hause geblieben.* (I had stayed home.)

Exercise 14-4

1. *er hat geschlagen*   *er hatte geschlagen*   *er wird geschlagen haben*
2. *sie haben gebracht*   *sie hatten gebracht*   *sie werden gebracht haben*

3. *es ist passiert*	*es war passiert*	*es wird passiert sein*
4. *sie ist gewesen*	*sie war gewesen*	*sie wird gewesen sein*
5. *du hast gehabt*	*du hattest gehabt*	*du wirst gehabt haben*
6. *ihr habt gegessen*	*ihr hattet gegessen*	*ihr werdet gegessen haben*
7. *Sie sind gekommen*	*Sie waren gekommen*	*Sie werden gekommen sein*
8. *wer ist gereist*	*wer war gereist*	*wer wird gereist sein*
9. *wir haben gesetzt*	*wir hatten gesetzt*	*wir werden gesetzt haben*
10. *ich habe gesehen*	*ich hatte gesehen*	*ich werde gesehen haben*

Chapter 15

Exercise 15-1

1. <u>*Hast*</u> *du zu Hause* <u>*bleiben müssen?*</u>
   (Did you have to stay at home?)
2. *Mein Vetter* <u>*hat*</u> *Klavier* <u>*spielen können.*</u>
   (My cousin could play the piano.)
3. <u>*Hat*</u> *er mit deiner Frau* <u>*tanzen dürfen?*</u>
   (Was he allowed to dance with your wife?)
4. *Der Lehrer* <u>*hat*</u> *lauter* <u>*sprechen sollen.*</u>
   (The teacher should have talked louder.)
5. *Wir* <u>*haben*</u> *Brot mit Käse* <u>*essen wollen*</u>
   (We have wanted to eat bread with cheese.)
6. *Ich* <u>*habe*</u> *viel* <u>*arbeiten müssen.*</u>
   (I have had to work a lot.)
7. *Die Mädchen* <u>*haben*</u> *Tennis* <u>*spielen können.*</u>
   (The boys could play tennis.)
8. <u>*Habt*</u> *ihr mit der Katze* <u>*spielen dürfen?*</u>
   (Were you allowed to play with the cat?)
9. *Die Männer* <u>*haben*</u> *weniger Bier* <u>*trinken sollen.*</u>
   (The men should have drunk less beer.)
10. <u>*Hat*</u> *sie Karl* <u>*kennen lernen wollen?*</u>
    (Did she want to meet Karl?)

Exercise 15-2

1. *Ich __werde__ nicht zu Hause __bleiben dürfen__.*
   (I will not be allowed to stay at home.)
2. *Diese Leute __werden__ mit dem Bus __fahren wollen__.*
   (These people will want to go by bus.)
3. *Warum __werde__ ich auf ihn __warten müssen__?*
   (Why will I have to wait for him?)
4. *Er __wird__ schnell __lernen können__.*
   (He will be able to learn quickly.)
5. *__Werdet__ ihr ihn __verstehen können__?*
   (Will you all be able to understand him?)
6. *__Werden__ Sie in Bonn __bleiben müssen__?*
   (Will you have to stay in Bonn?)
7. *Erik __wird__ mit Tina __tanzen wollen__.*
   (Erik will want to dance with Tina.)
8. *__Wirst__ du lauter __sprechen können__?*
   (Will you be able to speak louder?)
9. *Sie __wird__ nicht __mitgehen dürfen__.*
   (She won't be allowed to go along.)
10. *Ihr __werdet__ nicht mehr __arbeiten wollen__.*
    (You won't want to work anymore.)

Exercise 15-3

1. *er hat versprochen* (he has promised)
2. *er hat besucht* (he has visited)
3. *er hat verstanden* (he has understood)
4. *er hat ausgegeben* (he has spent)
5. *er hat verkauft* (he has sold)
6. *er ist abgefahren* (he has departed)
7. *er hat erwartet* (he has expected)
8. *er hat erkannt* (he has recognized)
9. *er hat bestellt* (he has ordered)
10. *er hat bekommen* (he has received)

Chapter 16

Exercise 16-1

1. _Dein_ Vater war im Wohnzimmer.
   (Your father was in the living room.)
2. Ich kenne _ihre_ Mutter. (I know her mother.)
3. Wir sahen _seinen_ Bruder im Theater.
   (We saw his brother at the theater.)
4. Der Franzose kaufte _unseren_ Volkswagen.
   (The Frenchman bought our Volkswagen.)
5. Wo ist _Ihr_ Vetter? (Where is your cousin?)
6. Das sind _meine_ Bücher. (Those are my books.)
7. Wo ist _ihr_ Haus? (Where is their house?)
8. Sind _eure_ Plätze gut? (Are your seats [in the theater] good?)
9. Karl besuchte _seinen_ Onkel in der Hauptstadt.
   (Karl visited his uncle in the capital city.)
10. Das ist ein Geschenk für _unsere_ Lehrerin.
    (That is a present for our teacher.)

Chapter 17

Exercise 17-1

1. Das Haus ist nicht klein, sondern groß.
2. Dieses Bild ist nicht hässlich, sondern hübsch.
3. Die Suppe ist nicht kalt, sondern heiß.
4. Oma ist nicht jung, sondern alt.
5. Ich hasse Karl nicht, sondern ich liebe ihn.
6. Er hat nicht viel Geld, sondern wenig Geld.
7. Der Film ist nicht lustig, sondern traurig.
8. Es ist nicht weiß, sondern schwarz.
9. Der Schüler ist nicht dumm, sondern klug.
10. Der Zug fährt nicht langsam, sondern schnell.

Exercise 17-2

1. Wie viel kostet ein _neuer_ Wagen?
2. Eine _hässliche_ Katze steht vor der Tür.
3. Das ist ein _interessanter_ Roman.
4. Der _deutsche_ Rennwagen ist sehr schnell.
5. Dein _weißes_ Kleid ist zu kurz.
6. Ich habe einen _braunen_ Hund.
7. Sie trägt eine _schöne_ Jacke.
8. Meine _neuen_ Freunde sind in Köln.
9. Kennst du diese _alte_ Frau?
10. Ein _junger_ Mann wartet auf uns.

Exercise 17-3

1. schlecht, schlechter, am schlechtesten
2. sauber, sauberer, am saubersten
3. groß, größer, am größten
4. hoch, höher, am höchsten
5. hübsch, hübscher, am hübschesten
6. faul, fauler, am faulsten
7. klein, kleiner, am kleinsten
8. laut, lauter, am lautesten
9. interessant, interessanter, am interessantesten
10. gern, lieber, am liebsten

Chapter 18

Exercise 18-1

1. Ich weiß nicht, wer das Fenster gebrochen hat.
   (I don't know who broke the window.)
2. Ich weiß nicht, wen Mutter besuchen will.
   (I don't know who Mother wants to visit.)
3. Ich weiß nicht, wann das Flugzeug fliegt.
   (I don't know when the plane leaves.)

4. *Ich weiß nicht, welches Hemd Jens haben möchte.*
   (I don't know which shirt Jens would like to have.)
5. *Ich weiß nicht, was für einen Wagen Vater gekauft hat.*
   (I don't know what kind of car Father bought.)

Exercise 18-2

1. *Wir sehen die Kinder in dem Garten.*
   (We see the children in the garden.)
2. *Die Zeitungen waren neben dem Heft.*
   (The newspapers were next to the book.)
3. *Vater ging langsam an die Tür.*
   (Father went slowly to the door.)
4. *Die Kinder laufen hinter das Haus.*
   (The children ran behind the house.)
5. *Mein Vetter sitzt neben seiner Frau.*
   (My cousin is sitting next to his wife.)
6. *Die Jungen spielen im Park.*
   (The boys play in the garden.)
7. *Er stellt die Vase auf das Klavier.*
   (He places the vase on the piano.)
8. *Was hängt über dem Tisch?*
   (What's hanging above the table?)
9. *Sie läuft in die Küche.* (She runs into the kitchen.)
10. *Wer steht an der Ecke?* (Who's standing on the corner?)

Chapter 19

Exercise 19-1

1.	*sein*	*sei*	*wäre*
2.	*ansehen*	*sehe an*	*sähe an*
3.	*warten*	*warte*	*wartete*
4.	*bekommen*	*bekomme*	*bekäme*
5.	*wissen*	*wisse*	*wüsste*
6.	*müssen*	*müsse*	*müsste*

7.	*kaufen*	*kaufe*	*kaufte*
8.	*trinken*	*trinke*	*tränke*
9.	*essen*	*esse*	*äße*
10.	*lernen*	*lerne*	*lernte*

Exercise 19-2

1. *Mutter sagte, dass unser alter Freund zu Besuch kommen werde (würde).* (Mother said that our old friend would come for a visit.)
2. *Mutter sagte, dass sie ihre neue Brille verloren habe (hätte).* (Mother said that she had lost her new glasses.)
3. *Mutter sagte, dass Jens seine Hausaufgaben machen solle (sollte).* (Mother said that Jens should do his homework.)
4. *Mutter sagte, dass es bald ein Gewitter geben werde (würde).* (Mother said there was going to be a thunderstorm soon.)
5. *Mutter sagte, dass Vater nicht mehr arbeiten könne (könnte).* (Mother said Father cannot work anymore.)

APPENDIX B

English-to-German Dictionary

Note that German nouns are followed by the following abbreviations: "m." stands for masculine (*der*), "f." stands for feminine (*die*), "n." stands for neuter (*das*), and "pl." stands for plural (*die*).

above all
vor allem, vor allen Dingen

actor/actress
Schauspieler/Schauspielerin, m./f.

after
nach

again
wieder

against
gegen, wider

airline ticket
Flugkarte, f.

airplane
Flugzeug, n.

airport
Flughafen, m.

alarm clock
Wecker, m.

almost
beinahe, fast

alone
allein

Alps
Alpen, pl.

already
schon

also, too
auch

aluminum
Aluminium, n.

always
immer

American
Amerikaner/Amerikanerin, m./f.

and
und

answer, to answer
Antwort, f., antworten

apartment
Wohnung, f.

ape, monkey
Affe, m.

apple
Apfel, m.

apple cake, tart
Apfelkuchen, m.

apprentice
Lehrling, m.

April
April, m.

area code
Vorwahl, f.

around
um

to arrive
ankommen

artist
Künstler/Künsterlin, m./f.

as, than
als

as if
als ob, als wenn

to ask (a question)
fragen

to ask, request
bitten

to assume
annehmen

at
an

at, by, at the house of
bei

at home
zu Hause

ATM (automatic teller machine)
Geldautomat, m.

attention
Achtung, f.

attic
Dachstube, f.

August
August, m.

aunt
Tante, f.

Austria
Österreich

autumn
Herbst, m.

back (part of the body)
Rücken, m.

back (direction)
zurück

bad
schlecht

to bake
backen

baker
Bäcker/Bäckerin, m./f.

bakery
Bäckerei, f.

bar
Lokal, n.

bathroom
Badezimmer, n.

bathtub
Badewanne, f.

Bavaria
Bayern

to be
sein

bear
Bär, m.

beard
Bart, m.

beautiful
schön

to be called
heißen

because
denn, weil

because of
wegen

to become, get
werden

bed
Bett, n.

bedroom
Schlafzimmer, n.

beer
Bier, n.

behind
hinter

Belgium
Belgien

to believe
glauben

to belong
gehören

better
besser

between
zwischen

big
groß

bike
Fahrrad, n.

billion
Milliarde, f.

birthday
Geburtstag, m.

black
schwarz

Black Forest
Schwarzwald, m.

blanket
Decke, f.

blind
blind

blouse
Bluse, f.

blue
blau

book
Buch, n.

bookcase
Bücherschrank, m.

boring
langweilig

born
geboren

bosom
Busen, m.

bottle
Flasche, f.

boy
Junge, m.

brass
Messing, n.

bread
Brot, n.

bread roll
Brötchen, n.

to break
brechen

to break to bits, destroy
zerbrechen

bridge
Brücke, f.

bright
hell

broken, wrecked
kaputt

brother-in-law
Schwager, m.

brothers and sisters
Geschwister, pl.

brown
braun

bull
Stier, m.

bus
Bus, m.

busy, occupied
besetzt

butcher
Fleischer/Fleischerin, m./f. or Metzger/Metzgerin, m./f.

butcher shop
Metzgerei, f.

butter
Butter, f.

to buy
kaufen

bye, so long
Tschüs

by no means
keineswegs

café
Café, n.

cage
Käfig, m

cake
Kuchen, m.

calendar
Kalender, m.

to call up
anrufen

calm, quiet
ruhig

can, to be able
können

capital city
Hauptstadt, f.

car
Wagen, m. or Auto, n.

car accident
Autounfall, m.

to carry
tragen

to catch
fangen

ceiling
Decke, f.

cellar
Keller, m.

chair
Stuhl, m.

chalk
Kreide, f

cheese
Käse, m.

chest
Brust, f.

chicken
Huhn, n.

child
Kind, n.

childhood
Kindheit, f.

chimney
Schornstein, m.

chimpanzee
Schimpanse, m.

chin
Kinn, n

chocolate
Schokolade, f.

city
Stadt, f.

class
Klasse, f.

clean (adj.)
sauber

to clear the table
abräumen

to climb
steigen

clock
Uhr, f.

to close
zumachen

closet
Schrank, m.

cloud
Wolke, f.

coast
Küste, f.

coat
Mantel, m.

coffee
Kaffee, m.

coin slot
Münzeinwurf, m.

cold (illness)
Erkältung, f.

cold (adj.)
kalt

colloquial language
Umgangssprache, f.

colony
Kolonie, f.

to come
kommen

to come along
mitkommen

company
Firma, f.

concert
Konzert, n.

to consist (of)
bestehen (aus)

cool
kühl

corner
Ecke, f.

correct
richtig

cousin
Kusine, f., Vetter, m.

cow
Kuh, f.

cream
Sahne, f.

crow
Krähe, f.

to cry
weinen

cup
Tasse, f.

dark
dunkel

date
Datum, n.

daughter
Tochter, f.

day
Tag, m.

day after tomorrow
übermorgen

day before yesterday
vorgestern

December
Dezember, m.

deer
Reh, n.

degree (temperature or angle)
Grad, m.

dentist
Zahnarzt/Zahnärztin, m./f.

to depart
abfahren

department store
Kaufhaus, n.

to destroy
zerstören

to dial, select
wählen

to die
sterben

diligent
fleißig

dining room
Esszimmer, n.

dirigible (zeppelin)
Luftschiff, n.

discotheque
Diskothek, f.

to dismiss
entlassen

divided by
geteilt durch

to divorce
scheiden

to do, make
machen

dolphin
Delphin, m.

door
Tür, f.

dress
Kleid, n.

drink, to drink
Getränk, n., trinken

drive, to drive
Fahrt, f., fahren

dry
trocken

duck
Ente, f.

during
während

during the day
tagsüber

each
jeder

eagle
Adler, m.

ear
Ohr, n.

early
früh

to eat
essen

economy
Wirtschaft, f.

eight
acht

eighteen
achtzehn

eighty
achtzig

elbow
Ellenbogen, m.

elephant
Elefant, m.

eleven
elf

elk
Elch, m.

embassy
Botschaft, f.

emperor
Kaiser, m.

empire
Reich, n.

energetic
energisch

Englishman/
Englishwoman
Engländer/Engländerin, m./f.

enough
genug

equal
gleich

euro (currency of the European Union)
Euro, m.

everyone, all
alle

everything, all
alles

exactly
genau

except
außer

exchange student
Austauschschüler/Austauschschülerin, m./f.

exercise
Übung, f.

exhibition
Ausstellung, f.

to expect, await
erwarten

eyes
Augen, pl.

fable
Fabel, f.

to fall
fallen

to fall asleep
einschlafen

family
Familie, f.

famous
berühmt

farm
Bauernhof, m.

fashionable
modisch

fast
schnell

February
Februar, m.

feminine
weiblich

fence
Zaun, m.

field
Feld, n.

fifteen
fünfzehn

fifty
fünfzig

to find
finden

finger
Finger, m.

fireplace
Kamin, m.

first
erste

five
fünf

floor
Boden, m., Fußboden, m.

floor lamp
Stehlampe, f.

floor tile
Fliese, f.

flower
Blume, f

to fly
fliegen

to fly gliders
segelfliegen

to follow
folgen

food
Essen, n.

foot
Fuß, m.

for
für

for a visit
zu Besuch

foreigner
Ausländer/Ausländerin, m./f

to forget
vergessen

forty
vierzig

four
vier

fourteen
vierzehn

fox
Fuchs, m.

Frenchman/
Frenchwoman
Franzose/Französin, m./f.

Friday
Freitag, m.

friend
Freund/Freundin, m./f.

from, of
von

from, out of
aus

from time to time
zeitweise

from where
woher

fruit torte
Obsttorte, f.

full, satiated
satt

funny
lustig

furious
wütend

game
Spiel, n.

garden
Garten, m.

gentleman
Herr, m.

Germany
Deutschland

to get, fetch
holen

to get away
abhauen

ghost
Gespenst, n.

gift
Geschenk, n.

giraffe
Giraffe, f.

girl
Mädchen, n.

girlfriend
Freundin, f.

to give
geben

gladly *gern, gerne*	**great-grandfather** *Urgroßvater, m.*	**hello** *hallo*
glass *Glas, n.*	**great-grandmother** *Urgroßmutter, f.*	**help, to help** *Hilfe, f., helfen*
glasses *Brille, f.*	**green** *grün*	**her (possessive adjective)** *ihr*
to go *gehen*	**groin** *Leiste, f.*	**here** *hier*
goat *Ziege, f.*	**guitar** *Gitarre, f.*	**to hide** *verbergen, verstecken (sich)*
gold *Gold, n.*	**hair** *Haar, n.*	**high** *hoch*
good *gut*	**half (adj.)** *halb*	**higher** *höher*
good-bye *auf Wiedersehen*	**half (noun)** *Hälfte, f.*	**High German** *Hochdeutsch*
good-bye (on the phone) *auf Wiederhören*	**hand** *Hand, f.*	**highway** *Autobahn, f.*
goose *Gans, f.*	**handsome** *hübsch*	**hip** *Hüfte, f.*
gorilla *Gorilla, m.*	**hang-gliding** *Drachenfliegen*	**hippo** *Nilpferd, n.*
grain *Getreide, n.*	**to happen** *geschehen, passieren*	**his** *sein*
gram *Gramm, n.*	**hare** *Hase, m.*	**holy** *heilig*
granddaughter *Enkelin, f.*	**to hate** *hassen*	**home(ward)** *nach Hause*
grandfather *Großvater, m.*	**have a good meal** *guten Appetit*	**homework** *Hausaufgabe, f.*
grandma *Oma, f.*	**he, it, m.** *er*	**honey** *Honig, m.*
grandmother *Großmutter, f.*	**head** *Kopf, m.*	**hopefully** *hoffentlich*
grandpa *Opa, m.*	**health** *Gesundheit, f.*	**horse** *Pferd, n.*
grandson *Enkel, m.*	**healthy** *gesund*	**hospital** *Krankenhaus, n.*
gray *grau*	**to hear** *hören*	**hot** *heiß*
great, crazy *toll*	**hedgehog** *Igel, m.*	**hot-air ballooning** *Ballonfahren*

hour
Stunde, f.

house
Haus, n.

how
wie

human
Mensch, m.

hundred
hundert

hungry
hungrig

I
ich

ice, ice cream
Eis, n.

ice skate
Schlittschuh laufen

idea
Idee, f.

if
wenn

illness
Krankheit, f.

important
wichtig

in, into
In

income
Einkommen, n.

in front of, before
vor

inn
Gasthof, m.

in spite of
trotz

instead of
anstatt

interesting
interessant

Internet
Internet, n.

iron
Eisen, n.

it
es, n.

Italy
Italien

itinerary
Reiseplan, m.

its
sein, ihr

jacket
Jacke, f.

jaguar
Jaguar, m.

January
Januar, m.

to jog
joggen

joyfulness
Fröhlichkeit, f.

judge
Richter, m.

July
Juli, m.

June
Juni, m.

just as
ebenso

key
Schlüssel, m.

to kill
erschlagen, töten

kilometer
Kilometer, m.

king
König, m.

kitchen
Küche, f.

kitchen range
Herd, m.

knee
Knie, n.

to know
wissen

to know, be acquainted with
kennen

lad
Knabe, m.

lady
Dame, f.

lake
See, m.

landscape
Landschaft, f.

language
Sprache, f.

last
letzte

late
spät

to laugh
lachen

laughter
Gelächter, n.

lazy
faul

lead
Blei, n.

to learn
lernen

leg
Bein, n.

to let
lassen

letter
Brief, m.

library
Bibliothek, f.

to like
gern haben, mögen

lion
Löwe, m.

little
klein

little (amount)	March	mother
wenig	*März, m.*	*Mutter, f.*
to live	market	mother-in-law
leben	*Markt, m.*	*Schwiegermutter, f.*
to live, reside	market square	mouth
wohnen	*Platz, m.*	*Mund, m.*
living room	to marry	movie theater
Wohnzimmer, n.	*heiraten*	*Kino, n.*
local call	masculine	Mr.
Ortsgespräch, n.	*männlich*	*Herr, m.*
lock, to lock	may, to be allowed	Mrs.
Schloss, n., zuschließen	*dürfen*	*Frau, f.*
loneliness	May	Ms.
Einsamkeit, f.	*Mai, m.*	*Frau, f.*
long	to mean	much
lang	*meinen*	*viel*
long-distance call	to meet	to murder
Ferngespräch, n.	*treffen*	*umbringen*
to look for	menu	museum
suchen	*Speisekarte, f.*	*Museum, n.*
to look up (in a book)	mess	music
nachschlagen	*Kram, m.*	*Musik, f.*
to lose	message	must, to have to
verlieren	*Botschaft, f.*	*müssen*
loud	midnight	my
laut	*Mitternacht, f.*	*mein*
love, to love	milk	naturally
Liebe, f., lieben	*Milch, f.*	*natürlich*
low	minute	nature
niedrig	*Minute, f.*	*Natur, f.*
Lower Saxony	mirror	near
Niedersachsen	*Spiegel, m.*	*nah*
Low German	mobile phone, cell phone	neck, throat
Plattdeutsch	*Mobiltelefon, n., Handy, n.*	*Hals, m.*
luck	Monday	to need
Glück, n.	*Montag, m.*	*brauchen*
magazine	money	neither . . . nor
Zeitschrift, f.	*Geld, n.*	*weder . . . noch*
man	more	nephew
Mann, m.	*mehr*	*Neffe, m.*
many	morning	nervous
mancher	*Morgen, m., Vormittag, m.*	*nervös*

never
niemals, nie

new
neu

news, message
Nachricht, f.

newspaper
Zeitung, f.

next
nächste

next to
neben

nice
nett

niece
Nichte, f.

nine
neun

nineteen
neunzehn

ninety
neunzig

no, not any
kein

no idea
keine Ahnung

no man's land
Niemandsland

nonetheless
nichtsdestoweniger

nonsense
Quatsch, m.

noon
Mittag, m.

no one
niemand

nose
Nase, f.

not
nicht

not any
keinerlei, gar kein

notebook
Heft, n.

nothing at all
gar nichts

novel
Roman, m.

November
November, m.

novice
Neuling, m.

now
jetzt

now and then
hin und wieder

nowhere
nirgendwo

nurse
*Krankenpfleger/Kranken-
pflegerin, m./ f.*

occur
passieren

October
Oktober, m.

office
Büro, n.

old-fashioned
altmodisch

old man, old woman
Alte, m./f.

on, onto
auf

once, one time
einmal

one
eins

one-way street
Einbahnstraße, f.

only
nur

on no account
keinesfalls

on the way
unterwegs

open
aufmachen

open (a book)
aufschlagen

opera
Oper, f.

or
oder

order, to order
Bestellung, f., bestellen

original
ursprünglich

oven
Ofen, m.

over, above
über

overseas call
Auslandsgespräch, n.

ox
Ochse, m.

palace
Schloss, n.

pants
Hose, f.

paper
Papier, n.

parents
Eltern, pl.

park
Park, m.

parliament
Bundestag, m.

parliament building in Berlin
Reichstag, m.

password
Passwort, n.

pastry shop
Konditorei, f.

pencil
Bleistift, m.

people
Leute, pl.

pepper
Pfeffer, m.

to perceive
empfinden

perfect
perfekt

physician
Arzt, m.

piano
Klavier, n.

to pick up
abholen

picture postcard
Ansichtskarte, f.

pig
Schwein, n.

pigeon, dove
Taube, f.

pin number (PIN)
Geheimnummer, f.

pipe
Pfeife, f.

plant, to plant
Pflanze, f., pflanzen

plate
Teller, m.

play (theater)
Schauspiel, n.

to play
spielen

play chess
Schach spielen

play Ping-Pong
Tischtennis spielen

please
bitte

to please
gefallen

pocket
Tasche, f.

pocket watch
Taschenuhr, f.

poetry
Poesie, f.

Poland
Polen

police officer
Polizist, m.

poor
arm

popular
populär

position
Stellung, f.

postcard
Postkarte, f.

post office, postal system
Post, f.

pound, half a kilo
Pfund, n.

preferably
lieber

prep school
Gymnasium, n.

pretty
hübsch

to prevail
überwiegen

price
Preis, m.

prince
Prinz, m.

princess
Prinzessin, f.

prize
Preis, m.

property
Eigentum, n.

to punish
bestrafen

pupil
Schüler, m.

purity
Reinheit, f.

to put down
hinlegen

quality
Qualität, f.

quarter
Viertel, n.

queen
Königin, f.

quiet
leise

racecar
Rennwagen, m.

radio
Radio, n.

railroad
Eisenbahn, f.

railroad car
Eisenbahnwagen, m.

railroad station
Bahnhof, m.

railway platform
Bahnsteig, m.

rain, to rain
Regen, m., regnen

rainy
regnerisch

rattlesnake
Klapperschlange, f.

to read
lesen

to receive, get
bekommen

red
rot

refrigerator
Kühlschrank, m.

relatives
Verwandten, pl.

repair, to repair
Reparatur, f., reparieren

restaurant
Restaurant, n.

rhinoceros
Nashorn, n.

rich
reich

right
recht

roof
Dach, n.

roof tile
Dachziegel, m.

rose
Rose, f.

rough
rauh, grob

rug, carpet
Teppich, m.

ruined, spoiled
verdorben

to run
laufen

Russian
Russe/Russin, m./f.

sad
traurig

saddle
Sattel, m.

sailor
Matrose, m.

salt
Salz, n.

Saturday
Sonnabend, m., Samstag, m.

sausage
Wurst, f.

to say
sagen

school
Schule, f.

school year
Schuljahr, n.

science
Wissenschaft, f.

sea
See, f.

seagull
Seemöwe, f.

seal
Seehund, m.

search, to search
Suche, f., suchen

to see
sehen

to sell
verkaufen

to send
schicken, senden

sentence
Satz, m.

September
September, m.

seven
sieben

seventeen
siebzehn

seventy
siebzig

she
sie

sheep
Schaf, n.

shirt
Hemd, n.

short
kurz

should, ought to
sollen

shoulder
Schulter, f.

to shout, scream
schreien

shower, to shower
Dusche, f., duschen

siblings
Geschwister, pl.

sick
krank

silver
Silber, n., silbern, adj.

simple
einfach

since
seit

to sing
singen

singer
Sänger/Sängerin, m./f.

sister
Schwester, f.

sister-in-law
Schwägerin, f.

to sit
sitzen

to sit down
sich hinsetzen

six
sechs

sixteen
sechzehn

sixty
sechzig

to ski
Ski laufen

skunk
Stinktier, n.

sleep, to sleep
Schlaf, m., schlafen

slow
langsam

smart
klug, intelligent

smoke, to smoke
Rauch, m., rauchen

smoking compartment
Raucherabteil, n.

smooth
glatt

snake
Schlange, f.

snow, to snow
Schnee, m., schneien

soccer
Fußball, m.

sofa, couch
Sofa, n.

soldier
Soldat/Soldatin, m./f.

something
etwas

son
Sohn, m.

soon
bald

sooner
eher

sour
sauer

Spaniard
Spanier/Spanierin, m./f.

sparrow
Sperling, m.

to speak
sprechen

to spend (money)
ausgeben

to spend (time)
verbringen

spoon
Löffel, m.

spring (season)
Frühling, m.

stairs
Treppe, f.

stamp, seal
Stempel, m.

to stand up, get up
aufstehen

to stand
stehen

to stay, remain
bleiben

to stay put, remain standing
stehen bleiben

steel
Stahl, m.

still
noch

stomach
Magen, m.

to stop, cease
aufhören

store
Laden, m., Geschäft, n.

stork
Storch, m.

storm
Sturm, m.

strong
stark

student
Student/Studentin, m./f.

to study
studieren or better: lernen

stupid
dumm

stupidity
Dummheit, f.

such a
solcher

summer
Sommer, m.

Sunday
Sonntag, m.

sunny
sonnig

swan
Schwan, m.

Sweden
Schweden

sweet
süß

to swim
schwimmen

Switzerland
Schweiz, f.

to take
nehmen

taste, to taste
Geschmack, m., schmecken

tea
Tee, m.

to teach
beibringen, unterrichten

teacher
Lehrer/Lehrerin, m./f.

telephone, to telephone
Telefon, n., telefonieren

telephone book
Telefonbuch, n.

telephone booth
Telefonzelle, f.

telephone operator
Vermittlung, f.

telephone receiver
Telefonhörer, m.

temperature
Temperatur, f.

ten
zehn

terrace
Terrasse, f.

terrible
furchtbar

terrific, glorious
herrlich

test
Prüfung, f.

to thank
danken

thank you
danke schön

that
jener

theater
Theater, n.

theater seat
Platz, m.

their
ihr

theory
Theorie, f.

there
da, dort

there is, there are
es gibt

they
sie (pl.)

thief
Dieb, m.

to think
denken

third
dritte

thirteen
dreizehn

thirty
dreißig

this
dieser

thousand
tausend

three
drei

through
durch

thumb
Daumen, m.

thunderstorm
Gewitter, n.

Thursday
Donnerstag, m.

tiger
Tiger, m.

time
Mal (how many times), n., Zeit, f.

tin
Zinn, n.

tired
müde

to
zu

today
heute

toe
Zehe, f.

tomato
Tomate, f.

tomorrow
morgen

too bad
schade

train
Zug, m.

translation
Übersetzung, f.

travel agency
Reisebüro, n.

trillion
Billion, f.

truth
Wahrheit, f.

try, to try
Versuch, m., versuchen

to try on
anprobieren

Tuesday
Dienstag, m.

Turkey
Türkei, f.

TV set
Fernseher, m.

twelve
zwölf

twenty
zwanzig

two
zwei, zwo

ugly
hässlich

uncle
Onkel, m.

under
unter

unfortunately
leider

United States
Vereinigten Staaten, pl.

unity
Einigkeit, f.

university
Universität, f.

to unlock
aufschließen

until, as far as
bis

to use
gebrauchen, benutzen

vegetables
Gemüse, n.

very
sehr

village
Dorf, n.

violin
Geige, f.

visit, to visit
Besuch, m., besuchen

voice
Stimme, f.

vulture
Geier, m.

to wait
warten

wall
Wand, f.

wall clock
Wanduhr, f.

walrus
Walross, n.

to want
wollen

war
Krieg, m.

warm
warm

to watch TV
fernsehen

water
Wasser, n.

we
wir

weak
schwach

to wear
tragen

weather
Wetter, n.

weather report
Wetterbericht, m.

Wednesday
Mittwoch, m.

week
Woche, f.

weekend
Wochenende, n.

weight
Gewicht, n.

well
Brunnen, m.

well
gut

wet
nass

whale
Wal(fisch), m.

what
was

what kind of
was für

when, whenever
wenn

where
wo

where (to)
wohin

which
welcher

whipped cream
Schlagsahne, f.

to whisper
flüstern

white
weiß

who
wer

whole
ganz

whom
wen, wem

whose
wessen

why
warum

wife
Ehefrau, Frau, f.

wild
wild

to win
gewinnen

wind
Wind, m.

window
Fenster, n.

wine
Wein, m.

winter
Winter, m.

with
mit

without
ohne

wolf
Wolf, m.

woman
Frau, f.

work, to work
Arbeit, f., arbeiten

wren
Zaunkönig, m.

wristwatch
Armbanduhr, f.

to write
schreiben

year
Jahr, n.

yellow
gelb

you (informal)
du

you (informal pl.)
ihr

you (formal)
Sie

young
jung

youngster
Jüngling, m.

your
dein (informal), *ihr* (informal plural), *Ihr* (formal)

you're welcome
bitte schön

youth
Jugend, f.

zero
Null, f.

Principal Parts of Irregular and Strong Verbs

This table contains the most frequently encountered irregular and strong verbs. Verbs with prefixes are included only when they are among those most frequently used. The present tense is provided only when there is an irregularity. In the present perfect tense, only the auxiliary *ist* will be indicated. Where it is not shown, assume that the auxiliary verb is *hat*.

Infinitive	Present	Past	Present Perfect	English
anfangen	fängt an	fing an	angefangen	begin, start
befehlen	befiehlt	befahl	befohlen	command
beginnen	beginnt	begann	begonnen	begin, start
booohroibon	booohroibt	booohriob	boschrioben	write
bitten	bittet	bat	gebeten	ask, beg
bleiben	bleibt	blieb	ist geblieben	remain, stay
brechen	bricht	brach	gebrochen	break
bringen	bringt	brachte	gebracht	bring
denken	denkt	dachte	gedacht	think
einladen	lädt ein	lud ein	eingeladen	invite
erscheinen	erscheint	erschien	ist erschienen	appear
essen	isst	aß	gegessen	eat
fahren	fährt	fuhr	ist gefahren	drive
fallen	fällt	fiel	ist gefallen	fall
finden	findet	fand	gefunden	find
fliegen	fliegt	flog	ist geflogen	fly

Infinitive	Present	Past	Present Perfect	English
fressen	frisst	fraß	gefressen	eat (used for animals)
geben	gibt	gab	gegeben	give
gehen	geht	ging	ist gegangen	go
geschehen	geschieht	geschah	ist geschehen	happen, occur
haben	hat	hatte	gehabt	have
halten	hält	hielt	gehalten	hold
heißen	heißt	hieß	geheißen	be called
helfen	hilft	half	geholfen	help
kennen	kennt	kannte	gekannt	know, be acquainted
kommen	kommt	kam	ist gekommen	come
lassen	lässt	ließ	gelassen	let
laufen	läuft	lief	ist gelaufen	run
lesen	liest	las	gelesen	read
liegen	liegt	lag	gelegen	lay
mögen	mag	mochte	gemocht	like
nehmen	nimmt	nahm	genommen	take
nennen	nennt	nannte	genannt	call
rennen	rennt	rannte	gerannt	run
rufen	ruft	rief	gerufen	call
schlafen	schläft	schlief	geschlafen	sleep
schlagen	schlägt	schlug	geschlagen	hit
schließen	schließt	schloss	geschlossen	close
schneiden	schneidet	schnitt	geschnitten	cut
schreiben	schreibt	schrieb	geschrieben	write
schwimmen	schwimmt	schwamm	ist geschwommen	swim
sehen	sieht	sah	gesehen	see
sein	ist	war	ist gewesen	be
singen	singt	sang	gesungen	sing
sitzen	sitzt	saß	gesessen	sit
sprechen	spricht	sprach	gesprochen	speak
springen	springt	sprang	ist gesprungen	jump, spring
stehen	steht	stand	gestanden	stand

Infinitive	Present	Past	Present Perfect	English
sterben	stirbt	starb	ist gestorben	die
tragen	trägt	trug	getragen	carry, wear
treffen	trifft	traf	getroffen	meet
trinken	trinkt	trank	getrunken	drink
tun	tut	tat	getan	do
verbieten	verbietet	verbat	verboten	forbid
vergessen	vergisst	vergaß	vergessen	forget
verlieren	verliert	verlor	verloren	lose
versprechen	verspricht	versprach	versprochen	promise
verstehen	versteht	verstand	verstanden	understand
wachsen	wächst	wuchs	ist gewachsen	grow
waschen	wäscht	wusch	gewaschen	wash
werden	wird	wurde	ist geworden	become, get
werfen	wirft	warf	geworfen	throw
wissen	weiß	wusste	gewusst	know
ziehen	zieht	zog	gezogen	pull
zwingen	zwingt	zwang	gezwungen	force

APPENDIX D

Verb Conjugation Tables

▼ **VERB TABLE 1. THE REGULAR PRESENT TENSE**

Pronoun	*spielen*	*fragen*	Pronoun	*spielen*	*fragen*
ich	spiele	frage	ihr	spielt	fragt
du	spielst	fragst	Sie	spielen	fragen
er/sie/es	spielt	fragt	sie	spielen	fragen
wir	spielen	fragen			

▼ **VERB TABLE 2. THE REGULAR PRESENT TENSE / STEM ENDING WITH –*T* OR –*D***

Pronoun	*warten*	*baden*	Pronoun	*warten*	*baden*
ich	warte	bade	ihr	wartet	badet
du	wartest	badest	Sie	warten	baden
er/sie/es	wartet	badet	sie	warten	baden
wir	warten	baden			

▼ **VERB TABLE 3. THE REGULAR PRESENT TENSE / STEM ENDING IN SIBILANT (-*S*, -*Z*, -*SS*, -*SS*)**

Pronoun	*reisen*	*duzen*	Pronoun	*reisen*	*duzen*
ich	reise	duze	ihr	reist	duzt
du	reist	duzt	Sie	reisen	duzen
er/sie/es	reist	duzt	sie	reisen	duzen
wir	reisen	duzen			

▼ **VERB TABLE 4. THE IRREGULAR PRESENT TENSE / VOWEL *E* CHANGES TO *I* OR *IE***

Pronoun	geben	sehen	Pronoun	geben	sehen
ich	gebe	sehe	ihr	gebt	seht
du	gibst	siehst	Sie	geben	sehen
er/sie/es	gibt	sieht	sie	geben	sehen
wir	geben	sehen			

▼ **VERB TABLE 5. THE IRREGULAR PRESENT TENSE / ADDITION OF UMLAUT**

Pronoun	fahren	laufen	Pronoun	fahren	laufen
ich	fahre	laufe	ihr	fahrt	lauft
du	fährst	läufst	Sie	fahren	laufen
er/sie/es	fährt	läuft	sie	fahren	laufen
wir	fahren	laufen			

▼ **VERB TABLE 6. THE PRESENT TENSE OF MODAL AUXILIARIES AND *WISSEN***

Pronoun	sollen	wollen	dürfen	können	mögen	wissen
ich	soll	will	darf	kann	mag	weiß
du	sollst	willst	darfst	kannst	magst	weißt
er/sie/es	soll	will	darf	kann	mag	weiß
wir	sollen	wollen	dürfen	können	mögen	wissen
ihr	sollt	wollt	dürft	könnt	mögt	wisst
Sie	sollen	wollen	dürfen	können	mögen	wissen
sie	sollen	wollen	dürfen	können	mögen	wissen

▼ **VERB TABLE 7. THE REGULAR PAST TENSE**

Pronoun	spielen	fragen	Pronoun	spielen	fragen
ich	spielte	fragte	ihr	spieltet	fragtet
du	spieltest	fragtest	Sie	spielten	fragten
er/sie/es	spielte	fragte	sie	spielten	fragten
wir	spielten	fragten			

▼ VERB TABLE 8. THE MIXED PAST TENSE

Pronoun	kennen	senden
ich	kannte	sandte
du	kanntest	sandtest
er/sie/es	kannte	sandte
wir	kannten	sandten
ihr	kanntet	sandtet
Sie	kannten	sandten
sie	kannten	sandten

Pronoun	kennen	senden	Pronoun	kennen	senden
ich	kannte	sandte	ihr	kanntet	sandtet
du	kanntest	sandtest	Sie	kannten	sandten
er/sie/es	kannte	sandte	sie	kannten	sandten
wir	kannten	sandten			

▼ VERB TABLE 9. THE IRREGULAR PAST TENSE

Pronoun	fahren	laufen	Pronoun	fahren	laufen
ich	fuhr	lief	ihr	fuhrt	lieft
du	fuhrst	liefst	Sie	fuhren	liefen
er/sie/es	fuhr	lief	sie	fuhren	liefen
wir	fuhren	liefen			

▼ VERB TABLE 10. THE IRREGULAR PAST TENSE OF MODAL AUXILIA- RIES AND *WISSEN*

Pronoun	sollen	wollen	dürfen	können	mögen	wissen
ich	sollte	wollte	durfte	konnte	mochte	wusste
du	solltest	wolltest	durftest	konntest	mochtest	wusstest
er/sie/es	sollte	wollte	durfte	konnte	mochte	wusste
wir	sollten	wollten	durften	konnten	mochten	wussten
ihr	solltet	wolltet	durftet	konntet	mochtet	wusstet
Sie	sollten	wollten	durften	konnten	mochten	wussten
sie	sollten	wollten	durften	konnten	mochten	wussten

▼ **VERB TABLE 11. THE PRESENT PERFECT TENSE OF REGULAR VERBS**

Pronoun	spielen	reisen
ich	habe gespielt	bin gereist
du	hast gespielt	bist gereist
er/sie/es	hat gespielt	ist gereist
wir	haben gespielt	sind gereist
ihr	habt gespielt	seid gereist
Sie	haben gespielt	sind gereist
sie	haben gespielt	sind gereist

▼ **VERB TABLE 12. THE PRESENT PERFECT TENSE OF IRREGULAR VERBS**

Pronoun	sprechen	gehen
ich	habe gesprochen	bin gegangen
du	hast gesprochen	bist gegangen
er/sie/es	hat gesprochen	ist gegangen
wir	haben gesprochen	sind gegangen
ihr	habt gesprochen	seid gegangen
Sie	haben gesprochen	sind gegangen
sie	haben gesprochen	sind gegangen

▼ **VERB TABLE 13. DOUBLE INFINITIVES IN THE PRESENT PERFECT TENSE**

Pronoun	können . . . sprechen	lassen . . . machen
ich	habe sprechen können	habe machen lassen
du	hast sprechen können	hast machen lassen
er/sie/es	hat sprechen können	hat machen lassen
wir	haben sprechen können	haben machen lassen
ihr	habt sprechen können	habt machen lassen
Sie	haben sprechen können	haben machen lassen
sie	haben sprechen können	haben machen lassen

▼ VERB TABLE 14. DOUBLE INFINITIVES IN THE PAST PERFECT TENSE

Pronoun	können . . . sprechen	lassen . . . machen
ich	hatte sprechen können	hatte machen lassen
du	hattest sprechen können	hattest machen lassen
er/sie/es	hatte sprechen können	hatte machen lassen
wir	hatten sprechen können	hatten machen lassen
ihr	hattet sprechen können	hattet machen lassen
Sie	hatten sprechen können	hatten machen lassen
sie	hatten sprechen können	hatten machen lassen

▼ VERB TABLE 15. THE PAST PERFECT TENSE OF REGULAR VERBS

Pronoun	spielen	reisen
ich	hatte gespielt	war gereist
du	hattest gespielt	warst gereist
er/sie/es	hatte gespielt	war gereist
wir	hatten gespielt	waren gereist
ihr	hattet gespielt	wart gereist
Sie	hatten gespielt	waren gereist
sie	hatten gespielt	waren gereist

▼ VERB TABLE 16. THE PAST PERFECT TENSE OF IRREGULAR VERBS

Pronoun	sprechen	gehen
ich	hatte gesprochen	war gegangen
du	hattest gesprochen	warst gegangen
er/sie/es	hatte gesprochen	war gegangen
wir	hatten gesprochen	waren gegangen
ihr	hattet gesprochen	wart gegangen
Sie	hatten gesprochen	waren gegangen
sie	hatten gesprochen	waren gegangen

▼ VERB TABLE 17. THE FUTURE TENSE

Pronoun	spielen	fahren
ich	werde spielen	werde fahren
du	wirst spielen	wirst fahren

Pronoun	spielen	fahren
er/sie/es	wird spielen	wird fahren
wir	werden spielen	werden fahren
ihr	werdet spielen	werdet fahren
Sie	werden spielen	werden fahren
sie	werden spielen	werden fahren

▼ VERB TABLE 18. DOUBLE INFINITIVES IN THE FUTURE TENSE

Pronoun	können . . . sprechen	lassen . . . machen
ich	werde sprechen können	werde machen lassen
du	wirst sprechen können	wirst machen lassen
er/sie/es	wird sprechen können	wird machen lassen
wir	werden sprechen können	werden machen lassen
ihr	werdet sprechen können	werdet machen lassen
Sie	werden sprechen können	werden machen lassen
sie	werden sprechen können	werden machen lassen

▼ VERB TABLE 19. THE PRESENT SUBJUNCTIVE I

Pronoun	spielen	haben	sein	kennen
ich	spiele	habe	sei	kenne
du	spielest	habest	seiest	konneot
er/sie/es	spiele	habe	sei	kenne
wir	spielen	haben	seien	kennen
ihr	spielet	habet	seiet	kennet
Sie	spielen	haben	seien	kennen
sie	spielen	haben	seien	kennen

▼ VERB TABLE 20. THE PRESENT SUBJUNCTIVE I OF MODAL AUXILIA-
RIES AND WISSEN

Pronoun	sollen	wollen	dürfen	können	mögen	wissen
ich	solle	wolle	dürfe	könne	möge	wisse
du	sollest	wollest	dürfest	könnest	mögest	wissest
er/sie/es	solle	wolle	dürfe	könne	möge	wisse

Pronoun	sollen	wollen	dürfen	können	mögen	wissen
wir	sollen	wollen	dürfen	können	mögen	wissen
ihr	sollet	wollet	dürfet	könnet	möget	wisset
Sie	sollen	wollen	dürfen	können	mögen	wissen
sie	sollen	wollen	dürfen	können	mögen	wissen

▼ VERB TABLE 21. SUBJUNCTIVE II

Pronoun	spielen	haben	sein	kennen
ich	spielte	hätte	wäre	kennte
du	spieltest	hättest	wärest	kenntest
er/sie/es	spielte	hätte	wäre	kennte
wir	spielten	hätten	wären	kennten
ihr	spieltet	hättet	wäret	kenntet
Sie	spielten	hätten	wären	kennten
sie	spielten	hätten	wären	kennten

▼ VERB TABLE 22. SUBJUNCTIVE II OF MODAL AUXILIARIES AND
  WISSEN

Pronoun	sollen	wollen	dürten	können	möchten	wissen
ich	sollte	wollte	dürfte	könnte	möchte	wüsste
du	solltest	wolltest	dürftest	könntest	möchtest	wüsstest
er/sie/es	sollte	wollte	dürfte	könnte	möchte	wüsste
wir	sollten	wollten	dürften	könnten	möchten	wüssten
ihr	solltet	wolltet	dürftet	könntet	möchtet	wüsstet
Sie	sollten	wollten	dürften	könnten	möchten	wüssten
sie	sollten	wollten	dürften	könnten	möchten	wüssten

▼ VERB TABLE 23. THE PASSIVE VOICE

Tense	sagen	lesen
Present	es wird gesagt	es wird gelesen
Past	es wurde gesagt	es wurde gelesen
Present Perfect	es ist gesagt worden	es ist gelesen worden
Past Perfect	es war gesagt worden	es war gelesen worden
Future	es wird gesagt werden	es wird gelesen werden

▼ **VERB TABLE 24. THE IMPERATIVE**

Command Type	spielen	geben	sein	werden
du	Spiel!	Gib!	Sei!	Werde!
ihr	Spielt!	Gebt!	Seid!	Werdet!
Sie	Spielen Sie!	Geben Sie!	Seien Sie!	Werden Sie!

▼ **VERB TABLE 25. TENSE FORMS WITH VERBS WITH SEPARABLE AND INSEPARABLE PREFIXES**

Tense	mitkommen	besuchen
Present	er kommt mit	er besucht
Past	er kam mit	er besuchte
Present Perfect	er ist mitgekommen	er hat besucht
Past Perfect	er war mitgekommen	er hatte besucht
Future	er wird mitkommen	er wird besuchen

Index